THE POLITICAL WORLDS OF
SLAVERY AND FREEDOM

The Nathan I. Huggins Lectures

THE POLITICAL WORLDS OF SLAVERY AND FREEDOM

Steven Hahn

HARVARD UNIVERSITY PRESS
Cambridge, Massachusetts, and London, England
2009

Library of Congress Cataloging-in-Publication Data

Hahn, Steven, 1951–
The political worlds of slavery and freedom / Steven Hahn.
p. cm.—(Nathan I. Huggins lectures)
Includes bibliographical references and index.
ISBN 978-0-674-03296-5 (alk. paper)
1. Slavery—Political aspects—United States—History.
2. Slaves—Emancipation—United States.   3. Slave insurrections—
United States—History—19th century.   4. African Americans—
Politics and government—19th century.   5. African Americans—
Politics and government—20th century.   6. Political participation—
United States—History—19th century.   7. Political participation—
United States—History—20th century.   8. Garvey, Marcus, 1887–1940.
9. Universal Negro Improvement Association.   10. Black
nationalism—United States—History—20th century.   I. Title.
E449.H15 2009
306.3′620973—dc22   2008036470

For Declan and Saoirse

Contents

PREFACE

The essays in this book, which span more than a century and a half of American history and range in their subjects from the emancipation process of the eighteenth and nineteenth centuries to the genealogies of Black Power in the twentieth, are nonetheless united by a number of themes and arguments. For the past two decades, I have been deeply interested in how African Americans, as slaves and freed people, practiced politics and expressed their changing political sensibilities even when they were excluded, as they usually were, from the formal arenas of southern and American political life. I have been interested, too, not only in how black politics gave shape to American society, but also in the new perspectives on political activity more generally that such an interest can encourage. Yet, as I reflect on my own work, and that of growing numbers of scholars and colleagues who share my concerns and projects, I am struck by how difficult it has been to unsettle well-entrenched frameworks of analysis and ways of seeing the past, by how resilient those frameworks and ways of seeing are, whatever contrary evidence is accumulated, and how readily that evidence is assimilated to familiar categories.

The Political Worlds of Slavery and Freedom, in effect, asks why this is, and thus it is about politics, and especially African American politics, in a double sense: about the political worlds of both history making and history writing. Why do we find it so difficult to follow the conceptual logic of episodes and materials we uncover even when scholars studying similar sorts of developments elsewhere in the world have already paved the way? Why are there interpretations we are reluctant to embrace even when the empirical evidence invites us to do so? And why are there subjects we can so easily avoid or disown, even when it is clear that they are of genuine historical significance? These issues and questions arise in relation to every field of historical (indeed scholarly) study, but they seem to have a special salience in the field of African American history in good part because the stakes of meaning are so high.

How might this become manifest? Several years ago, when I visited the New-York Historical Society's excellent exhibit Slavery in New York, I was struck as much by the reactions of those in attendance as by the powerful artifacts on display. It was apparent that few of the attendees had any idea that New York had a direct relationship with slavery, let alone that slavery was so important to New York's early development. Most were simply stunned. It was a remarkable educational moment. Yet, as I left the exhibit, I kept wondering what might be done with this knowledge and the challenges it posed to our understanding of the country's past. After all, historians have long recognized that slavery had a legal basis in all the European colonies of North America and, for a time, in all of the states of the United States. And in recent years they have come to demonstrate how hard it was to rid any jurisdiction of slavery, no matter how marginal slaves and slavery may have appeared, and how protracted the process of emancipation turned out to be.

Still, the general accounts of the nation's social and political history barely seem to have registered or attempted to pursue the implications. To a certain extent this is because much of the relevant new scholarship has been produced by historians of the eighteenth century and early national period, whereas the politics of slavery is often written by historians of the nineteenth century; plainly, they are not communicating very well. Even more consequentially, our discoveries about slavery's wide expanse and prolonged demise disrupt, perhaps in ways that are not very welcome, models of American political conflict that have been in place since before the Civil War itself. What would it mean, in political and interpretive terms, to recognize that slavery had a foothold and that slaves were to be found—working, fleeing, hiding, organizing—throughout America until the Union was dissolved? What would it mean for our sense of "sectional conflict" and for the interactions of people of African descent who were enslaved, free, and in a nether zone between slavery and freedom? The first essay takes up these questions, exploring what I regard as an extended emancipation process and the new fields of African American politics to which it may alert us.

Historians interested in slave emancipation in the United States have, of course, focused chiefly on the Civil War era and often emphasized features of that process—the explosive violence and destruction, the military and political defeat of the slaveholders—that may have set it apart from other emancipations in

the Americas and lent it a revolutionary character—
that is, with the acknowledged exception of Saint
Domingue (Haiti). There slavery was also destroyed
in what turned into a bloody civil war. There slaveholding rulers were also dispatched militarily and
politically. And in both Saint Domingue and the
Civil War-era United States slaves came to be centrally involved in the struggle. Yet, although what the
slaves did in Saint Domingue is almost universally
interpreted as a rebellion-turned-revolution—indeed,
the only successful one we know of in modern history—what the slaves did in the U.S. South, impressive and significant as it is recognized to have been,
is virtually never interpreted as a rebellion-turned-
anything. Rebellion, in fact, has been almost universally denied or rejected, despite the many thousands
of slaves who, by their actions, helped turn the Civil
War against slavery and secure the defeat of their
owners. Why has rebellion been so easy to ignore or
disown? Is it because of how we understand slaves in
political terms? Is it because of our discomfort with
the very idea of black rebellion, or of rebellion as an
aspect of black politics? The second essay explores
these problems, asking if we may have missed one of
history's great slave rebellions and why.

The African American struggle to define a meaningful freedom after the abolition of slavery has emerged as one of the most riveting, and unfinished, sagas in all of American history. And enormous attention has been devoted to studying both the repression and discrimination inflicted on freed black Americans and their astonishing efforts, chiefly through the developing Civil Rights movement, to battle for equality and opportunity. But there have been other movements that attracted and mobilized large numbers—perhaps even more—people of African descent that have been either overlooked or consciously ignored.

One of them is the Universal Negro Improvement Association, organized by Marcus Garvey and his supporters in the 1910s and 1920s, which cast long political and intellectual shadows. When I was finishing my last book and increasingly interested in the UNIA (it was a political experience that seemed to encompass the Great Migration, North and South), I was very much surprised to learn that only a limited secondary literature was to be found; and there was almost nothing on the UNIA's grassroots history. I had become curious, less about Garvey himself than about his many followers: Who were they? Where did they live and how did they earn their livelihoods? What did they hear and why did they join, or support, the UNIA? What did they think the movement was all about, and what happened to them and their ideas after Garvey's own demise? I discovered very few conjectures, let alone answers. How is it that historians interested in all manner of black "agency" and forms of "resistance" could be so uninterested in what was an immense international as well as national phenomenon? What has made Garvey and the UNIA seem either so repellent or so inconsequential? Why has this history remained so hidden from us? These are the issues I examine in the third, and final, essay, suggesting that the UNIA may have been part of a wider and deeper black political underground—especially during the period from emancipation until World War II—that we have still to excavate.

The historical moments and episodes covered in *The Political Worlds of Slavery and Freedom* offer, I believe and hope, a number of challenges to how we have come to approach American and African American history. And they suggest, at the very least, that we may wish to interrogate many of our assumptions about the dynamics of struggle and aspiration in which African Americans have engaged. History writing tends to place great emphasis on the ideals and goals—most harking back to the revolutionary decades of the eighteenth century—that black and white

Americans together embraced; and it has lent great moral power and political legitimacy to African Americans fighting for freedom and equality because those fights appear to envision a shared future and because they demand that Americans live up to their principles.

Beyond doubt, there is much to be said for this view, especially when we look at the lives, words, and projects of mainstream leaders. Yet, having spent more than twenty years trying to recover something of the grassroots experiences, practices, and sensibilities of African Americans as they endured and tried to shape their enslavement, their transition out of slavery, their encounters with paramilitarism and official repression, and their migrations across many miles and many different social circumstances—as they were involved in history making—I have been impressed by other ideals and goals that emerged, not in response to the failure of their battles for freedom, equality, and inclusion, but organically from their own histories and in complex relation to those battles. Chief among them were self-determination, self-governance, and self-defense, which, of course, had their own character and logic as to time and place.

There is a growing and increasingly sophisticated historical literature, particularly focused on the local histories of the mid-twentieth century (dealing variously with Black Power, the Black Panthers, the Deacons for Defense, Robert Williams, urban politics, and political economy), that takes the political tendencies of self-determination and self-defense seriously, and we can hope that it will be read thoughtfully. It will afford us both a deeper sense of the cultural and political divisions that have developed in our society, and a more fruitful way of imagining how those divisions may nourish, rather than undermine, our future. I would like *The Political Worlds of Slavery and Freedom* to serve as a small contribution to this possibility.

The Political Worlds of
Slavery and Freedom

"Slaves at Large"

*The Emancipation Process and the
Terrain of African American Politics*

When Lewis Garrard Clarke, who was born a slave in
early nineteenth-century Kentucky, crossed the Ohio
River in making his escape from captivity, he "trem-
bled all over with deep emotion," being "on what was
called free soil, among people who had no slaves."
But when Clarke arrived in nearby Cincinnati, he saw
"several times a great slave dealer from Kentucky,
who knew me," and "was very careful to give him
a wide berth." Soon concluding that "the *spirit* of
slaveholding was not all South of the Ohio River,"
Clarke determined to take the advice of a former
slave he met, who "urged" him to "go up the river to
Portsmouth, then take the canal for Cleveland, and
cross over to Canada." This time, after boarding a
vessel on Lake Erie and then stepping ashore in On-
tario, Clarke exclaimed, "sure enough I AM FREE," and

later found "a great deal of truth" in the observation of a Canadian employer that "there was no 'free state' in America, all were *slave* states—bound to slavery, and the slave could have no asylum in any of them."[1]

Clarke was hardly alone among fugitive slaves in wondering about the true borders of slavery in the antebellum United States. Fleeing into the northern states, many found that they "were still in an enemy's land," that slaveholders roamed the streets in search of their property with the sanction of local and federal authorities, that the "northern people are pledged . . . to keep them in subjection to their masters," and that even "in sight of the Bunker Hill Monument . . . no law" offered them protection. The fugitive Thomas Smallwood spoke bitterly of abolitionists who "would strenuously persuade" runaways "to settle in the so-called *Free States*"; they apparently did not recognize "the influence that slavery had over the entire union." For him and for so many others who attempted to flee their enslavement, true freedom beckoned only in Canada, Britain, or some other "entirely foreign jurisdiction." "When I arrived in the city of New York," Moses Roper remembered, "I thought I was free; but learned I was not." He quickly moved into the surrounding countryside, up the Hudson River to Poughkeepsie, on to Vermont,

New Hampshire, and Boston. It was all the same, and before long "two colored men informed me that a gentleman had been inquiring for a person whom, from the description, I knew to be myself." Roper "secreted" himself for several weeks, until he could get passage on a ship to Liverpool, where he finally felt that he had "escaped from the cruel bondage of slavery."[2]

The harrowing stories of fugitive slaves, inside and outside the territories of formal enslavement, in transit out of bondage and in search of new and secure lives in freedom, have long been told. And they are meant chiefly to remind us that racism has known no sectional boundaries in the United States, nor has it been an excrescence only of slavery and slave society. Racism and its institutional manifestations—repression, exclusion, segregation, disfranchisement—seem to be enlivened by freedom, we have learned, much as fire is by oxygen. Yet the narratives and autobiographies of the fugitives themselves often have a fundamentally different point to make: not that racism thrived on both sides of the border of slavery and freedom, but that the border itself was illusory and indistinct. That point, if taken seriously, does more than dramatize the challenges faced by slaves and fugitives; it disrupts one of the most deeply entrenched perspectives on America's past—a perspective that has been central and almost universally accepted in interpretive accounts, and that concerns the process by which slavery was abolished and the relationship between slave emancipation and the Civil War.

So far as one can see in the scholarly and popular literature, two discrete emancipations occurred in the United States: one—what the historian Arthur Zilversmit has called the "first emancipation"—that abolished slavery in New England and the Middle Atlantic states, and, together with the Northwest Ordinance of 1787, created a free-labor zone that has long been known as "the North"; and another, an emancipation that commenced in the heat of the Civil War, that was completed with the ratification of the Thirteenth Amendment to the Constitution in December 1865, and that abolished slavery in what has long been known as "the South."[3]

But the distinction drawn here is not merely chronological, acknowledging the many decades between the first emancipation and the second; it is also, and more significantly, a qualitative distinction. For, as is commonly noted, the first emancipation took place in areas of the country in which there were relatively few slaves and slave owners and in which slavery itself seemed to be peripheral to social and economic reproduction, whereas the second emancipation took place in areas in which there were a great many slaves and slave owners and in which slavery was fundamental to social and political organization. Thus, the first emancipation, in this reckoning, established the basic division of sectional conflict, which in turn led (in any one of a number of scenarios) to disunion and the Civil War, and then eventuated in the second—and far more substantial and revolutionary—emancipation, one that appears to stand almost alone on the world stage in its sweep and consequences.[4]

This is all well and good, and it has mapped the narrative of the nation's early history that we customarily present. The first emancipation generally gets, at most, passing reference, chiefly in association with the repercussions of the American Revolution. It is then largely forgotten as we consider the developing conflict between the "free-labor" North and the "slave-labor" South and come to focus on the main (and in some representations the only) emancipation event, that of the 1860s. The problem is that this perspective no longer comports very well with what we have been learning—or at least with the implications of what we have been learning—over the past decade or so about slavery in the eighteenth century, about the emancipation process in New England, the Middle Atlantic, and the Old Northwest, and about the political and juridical bases of slavery in antebellum America. For what we have been learning suggests that a major reconceptualization of emancipation may be in order: that we ought to imagine emancipation not as two relatively discrete phases, but rather as a connected and remarkably protracted process, one far more protracted than anywhere else in the Americas. And once we do this, we may begin to look at the social and political history of the nineteenth century in very different ways.

In recent years a rich scholarly literature that builds on the foundational work of African American historians such as Lorenzo Greene has offered powerful challenges to our understanding of the universe and significance of North American slavery in the eighteenth and early nineteenth centuries. It has demonstrated that slavery established important footholds in northern as well as southern colonies from early on in various European colonial projects, that slavery became more entrenched everywhere over the course of the eighteenth century, and that even in New England slavery was integral to social, economic, and political development. Although few whites overall in New England and the Middle Atlantic owned slaves, slave ownership there, as elsewhere in the Americas, was concentrated disproportionately among those most involved in commercial and political activities: slave owning was most common among merchants, shippers, lawyers, artisans, public officials, and, at times, planters (such as those in Narragansett, Rhode Island). In some places perhaps half (or more) of the people in these occupations owned slaves. The distribution of slave ownership may, in fact, say most about the large proportion of the free population of the Northeast during this period that was involved peripherally, if at all, in the Atlantic economy.[5]

As is well known, an abolition process did begin during the Revolutionary era owing to the ideological and cultural currents of the times and to the disruptions and demands of the anticolonial struggles. It ultimately moved through eight of the original states. Less well known, and certainly less well appreciated, are both the gradual nature of the process and the hedged and ambiguous world of "freedom" into which emancipated slaves were ushered. Between 1780 and 1804 the states of Pennsylvania, Rhode Island, Connecticut, New York, and New Jersey enacted "emancipation" statutes. But not one of those statutes freed any slave. They provided instead for the emancipation of the *children* of those who were en-slaved (*post-nati* emancipation, as it is known), and only when they reached a certain point in their adult-hood: age twenty-one, twenty-five, or twenty-eight, depending on the state and their gender. Slave own-ers thereby received the most productive fruits of slave labor as compensation for the eventual loss of their property and were often relieved of responsibil-ity for their slaves once those slaves gained freedom.[6]

In Massachusetts and New Hampshire slavery's end appeared less gradual though at the same time more confusing, accomplished chiefly through judi-cial interpretation of state constitutions that, in fact, made no mention of slavery. Thus, people officially acknowledged as slaves could be found in several northern states well into the nineteenth century—in New Jersey as late as 1860—and it would be decades before these states finally got around to pronouncing slavery legally dead. New York did so in 1827, New Jer-sey in 1846, Pennsylvania in 1847, Connecticut in 1848, and New Hampshire in 1857.[7]

Yet what can be seen as an extended emancipation process by no means ran its course in New England and the Middle Atlantic. Commencing with the up-heavals of the Revolutionary years and lasting until, at least, the second decade of the nineteenth century,

the Chesapeake and the Upper South more generally saw private manumissions on a substantial scale,
which greatly enlarged the size of the free black population there and began to undermine slavery as
an institution in Delaware and parts of Maryland.
By 1810 people of African descent who had gained
their freedom represented more than 10 percent of
the black population in the Upper South, and they
found niches in rural as well as urban areas, establishing a distinctive social and political context for
both slavery and emancipation. By the time of the
Civil War, half of the African Americans in Maryland
and more than 90 percent of those in Delaware were
free.[8]

The prospects and discourse of emancipation resonated further still. In the early 1830s, amid heightened social and political tensions, the legislatures of
Maryland and Virginia publicly considered and debated the wisdom of the gradual abolition of slavery
coupled with colonization: that is to say, abolition
accompanied by the forced exile of the blacks who
were freed, which would remain the touchstone of
emancipationist thought and policy until the middle
of the Civil War. The event was of special meaning
in Virginia because there it was surrounded by Nat
Turner's rebellion in Southampton County (1831) and

by the political unrest of nonslaveholders who were demanding limits to the prerogatives of large slaveholders in the eastern section of the state (1829–31), and because Virginia held more slaves than any other state in the Union—and would continue to do so until the end. Although the debates convinced most legislators that emancipation was unworkable and posed unacceptable threats to the social order, the final vote on the expediency of action against slavery was fairly close and received overwhelming support from those representing the Shenandoah Valley and the state's west.[9]

At the same time, this emancipation process had complex and contradictory aspects, not all developing along new "sectional" lines. We, of course, know full well that during the very years that slavery was being attacked and weakened in New England, the Middle Atlantic, and parts of the border South, it was also expanding into Kentucky and Tennessee, into the Deep South states of Alabama and Mississippi, and, with the Louisiana Purchase, into the trans-Mississippi West. But we must not forget about a variety of practices and developments north of the Ohio River and the Mason-Dixon line that enabled slavery to establish or maintain a footing in the states and territories where, ostensibly, the institution had

means, for removing Indians from areas of rapid settlement, and for imagining an empire that might
have included Mexico, Central America, and Cuba.
Consider, for example, the presidents under whose
auspices the United States purchased the Louisiana
Territory from France (Thomas Jefferson), acquired
Florida from Spain (James Monroe), forcibly resettled
Indians west of the Mississippi (Andrew Jackson),
annexed the Texas Republic (John Tyler), waged war
against Mexico, and obtained the territories of the
southwest and northwest (James K. Polk). They were
slaveholders, and slaveholding planters, all! And they
presided over what the historian Don Fehrenbacher
has aptly termed a "slaveholding republic."[13]

☙❧

If we can think about American slavery and emancipation in this way—if, that is, we can think about
slavery as national (and perhaps the United States in
its early decades as a slave society in transition) and
about emancipation as an ongoing process initiated
during the Revolutionary era, although one that was
uneven, haphazard, and nonlinear—we may discover
new interpretive possibilities, or at least a new orientation and set of perspectives on American development.

been rendered illegal. Slaveholders, some of them of
French extraction, were in the Illinois Country at the
time the Northwest Ordinance established a framework for governing the newly created Northwest Territory and, at least in theory, prohibited "slavery and
involuntary servitude" within the jurisdiction.[10] They
were able to wield power in subsequent territorial
legislatures because the territorial governor chose to
interpret the ordinance (with the tacit acquiescence
of the Washington administration) as forbidding the
further introduction of slaves rather than as emancipating those already there. These slaveholders pressed
to legalize slavery when the state constitutions of
Ohio, Indiana, and Illinois were drawn (and nearly
succeeded); they tried to call constitutional conventions thereafter to make relevant revisions; and they
availed themselves of long-term indentures that had
passed emancipationist scrutiny and provided an ongoing basis for forced labor. All the while, slaves
worked in lead mines, on farms, in iron foundries,
and as domestics as far north and west as Wisconsin
and Iowa, and they appear to have been hired in
southern Illinois, Indiana, and Ohio from slaveholders in Kentucky, and in western Pennsylvania from
slaveholders in Virginia.[11]

The number of slaves in New England, the Middle

Atlantic, and the lower Midwest did dwindle between 1790 and 1850. Yet, just as slaves disappeared officially from the census and tax rolls for those states, the status of slavery gained a renewed lease on life. In *Prigg v. Pennsylvania* (1842), with Justice Joseph Story of Massachusetts writing the majority opinion, the U.S. Supreme Court not only confirmed the right of recaption that the Fugitive Slave Law of 1793 had established; it also determined that slaveholders were effectively protected by the laws of their own states when they sought to apprehend runaways in states where slavery had been outlawed—thus giving slavery a legal basis virtually everywhere. The Fugitive Slave Law of 1850 lent slaveholders greater leverage still by requiring the appointment of federal commissioners to adjudicate cases, by offering commissioners and judges monetary incentives to remand fugitives to slavery, by punishing federal officials who refused to participate or citizens who sought to aid or harbor fugitives, and by denying fugitives jury trials. The *Dred Scott* decision of 1857, which ruled on the civil and political standing of African Americans in the United States and on whether the federal territories could be closed to slavery, and the slave transit cases that considered whether slaveholders could legally travel with their slaves through "free" states and were

making their way toward the Supreme C ened to go even further: they opened the ritories to slaveholders and implicitly ra about the constitutionality of emancipa in the states themselves. Thus, as slaves officially in the states of what we call the were appearing unofficially as fugitives fr of the South.[12]

The picture that can be sketched, the in which slavery—for the duration of th period—was national rather than sectio freedom for African Americans was h gent and to be found in discrete geop and in which abolition and antislavery carnations, were struggling, with succ ures, to limit the prerogatives of sla build constituencies of support. Acc holders and their allies wielded enorm the federal government, dominating the Supreme Court, and the diplomatic the 1850s, and having enough muscl chiefly through their influence in t Party, to defeat unfavorable policies v to achieve what they desired. They we responsible for expanding the geogr the United States through military

For one thing, we may come to think more fully about slavery, emancipation, and, eventually, the Civil War not so much as manifestations of fundamentally antagonistic forms of social and productive organization or of "irrepressible conflicts" between a "free-labor North" and a "slave-labor South," but rather as central aspects of American state formation: as central to the rise, developing institutional capacity, claims to authority, and consolidation of a nation-state. It is true, of course, that historians now tend to associate slavery in the Americas with a vague notion of "modernity"; and there surely can be no question that slave systems, in their plantation contexts, did become enormous sources of capital accumulation and, in some quarters, bourgeois empowerment. Yet it would, at the same time, be difficult to identify anything resembling a modern nation-state that included a significant regime of slavery within its borders. Indeed, the United States stands alone among modern republics in the duration of its direct coexistence with slavery, although the many conflicts that jeopardized the viability of the republic during these eight decades of coexistence demonstrated how tough it would be to accommodate politically the forms of power—notably the personal and particularistic sovereignties—that attached to slaveholding.[14]

The crisis of the 1850s, therefore, was not simply another round in the contest over whose vision of state and local authority would prevail. It was no longer a battle between expansive and restricted conceptions of federal power. It instead unleashed a full-out struggle over who would control the state itself (that is, the offices and apparatus of the national government). On the one side, Republicans promised to keep slavery and slaveholders out of the federal territories in the West; on the other, slaveholding Democrats called for a federal slave code to enforce the dictates of the *Dred Scott* decision. Either way, the goal was to claim and wield, not limit, state power. When the slaveholders saw the struggle as lost, many of them quickly rebelled against the federal government and attempted to devise a political solution of their own. But the tensions between the logics of state building and of slaveholding would not end with secession; they would bedevil the Confederacy as well.[15]

Understanding slavery and emancipation in the United States chiefly in relation to state formation rather than to "sectionalism," moreover, may enable us to get a deeper sense of the connections between an array of conflicts—many involving questions of power and authority—that erupted throughout the country, and along an assortment of "borders" (not just North-South), during the antebellum period. What we have come to call the "market revolution" and the cultures increasingly associated with it did not merely divide the nation in two; they fractured states, regions, and localities—North, South, and West— over issues of money, credit, social reform, gender relations, religious belief, and state power, creating sympathies and alliances that traversed the familiar sectional lines and often influenced partisan loyalties. They can help us understand reinvigorations of patriarchalism, often stirred by evangelical enthusiasm, in many parts of the country. They can help us understand how radical workers in New York City could, in the 1840s, identify with the views of John C. Calhoun. They can help us understand how antiabolitionist mobs could surface as late as 1860 in the "burnt-over district" of upstate New York, and how newspaper editors in major northern cities could sympathize with southern slaveholders and even defend slavery. They can help us understand the ferocity of wartime draft riots in New York and Pennsylvania. And they can help us recognize what an enormous and complex task it was for the Republican Party to construct a winning antislavery coalition.[16]

The imperial impulse of the era similarly turns our attention away from the axis of North and South, this time toward that of East and West: toward the borders of Texas and Mexico, of Oregon and Canada, of Kansas and the Southwest. It reminds us both how important these borders were to the struggles over slavery and how little attention they normally receive in the telling of the Civil War and its aftermath. There are few studies of the war or Reconstruction that have much to say about the trans-Mississippi West or about the populations to be found there, including Indians, and about how they figure in the meaning of these great events—and they figure significantly.[17] It is, in fact, arguable that one of the most far-reaching results of the Civil War and emancipation was the opening of the trans-Mississippi West to new patterns of social and economic development, to the incorporation of local elites and subject populations, and to federal initiatives and activities that would lay the groundwork for the future. And, as it turns out, the advanced sections of the rural and extractive economies there came to depend on the wage and contract labor not of the white native-born, but of immigrants from countries that were emancipating their own peasantries through the abolition of servile ties, the commodification of land and labor, or both. One thinks, in this connection, of China, southwest Asia, and southern Europe, and of the Chinese, East Indians, Italians, Basques, and Greeks.[18]

The global circulation of newly emancipated Asian and European peasants thereby gave shape to the economies of the postbellum West as well as to those elsewhere in the postemancipation Americas (Cuba, Trinidad, the Guianas, and Brazil, for example). And it suggests clearly that emancipation and its consequences were international in their unfolding and significance.[19] But the "two emancipations" and "sectional conflict" models that have dominated the historiography of the United States may well have prevented us from taking the full measure of this. "Atlantic" history and "transnational" perspectives have been embraced chiefly by early Americanists rather than by those writing on the nineteenth century. Even the sparkling works on the comparative history of slavery of the past half century generally focus on the second emancipation of the Civil War era as if it were disconnected from the first, and they draw comparative conclusions accordingly.[20]

The difficulty with such an approach is that a crucial international dynamic of change, communication, and influence may then be overlooked. The emancipation process that commenced during the American Revolutionary era was a development of immense international significance. It saw the first laws providing for the abolition of slavery in the Atlantic world; it played a role in the outcome of the Revolutionary War and certainly in the subsequent efforts to build a United States; and its currents were to be felt in Saint Domingue during the 1790s in what became the Haitian Revolution.[21] The Haitian Revolution, in turn, had an enormous, though still underappreciated, influence on American politics in the 1790s and early 1800s because it intensified the struggle between Federalists and Republicans, terrified slaveholders and other major propertied interests, and produced thousands of exiles (white, black, and colored), many of whom arrived in American ports from Philadelphia to New Orleans on the eve of the large-scale migration of slavery and the plantation system into the interior of the Deep South. Most important, the French defeat at the hands of Saint Domingue's slaves and free people of color ended Napoleon's dream of a New World empire and led to the sale of Louisiana: the event that, perhaps more than any other, shaped the course of American history in the nineteenth century, including the course of slavery and emancipation.[22]

This became evident in well-known ways beginning with the contest over the admission of Missouri to the Union in 1819–21. But it also became evident when, owing in part to the abolition of slavery in Mexico, Americans in Texas, on the border of Louisiana (many of them slaveholders), rebelled, established an independent republic, and opened the question of Texas annexation. In the meantime, the struggles of British abolitionists at home and, especially, of slaves in the British colonial possessions of the Caribbean—which exploded in 1816 in Barbados, in 1823 in Demerara, and in 1831–32 in Jamaica—set the path, first of amelioration and then of abolition, in the British colonies during the 1830s. The shock waves were widely felt, particularly in the United States, not least because American slaveholders feared that the British might coax the Texans to abolish slavery in return for political and material support.[23]

More consequential still, the success that many ex-slaves in the British possessions (notably in Jamaica) had in resisting plantation labor, which helped send the island's sugar economy into steep decline, convinced many American slaveholders that emancipation was a failure (all the more so in light of the convulsive Haitian Revolution), whether gradual, compensated, or both.[24] Slavery and emancipation in the United States, that is, not only developed in an international context, but also shaped and were shaped by that context. And it is likely that the "two emancipations" and "sectional conflict" models of analysis have made this very difficult to see, because they have allowed the focus of study to be exclusively on the United States.

శాస

For the moment, it may be useful to place special emphasis on the implications of the "two emancipations" and "sectional conflict" models for our sense of African American politics in the tumultuous period between the Revolution and the Civil War, because we have come to conceive of those politics in an overly segmented way. Indeed, scholarly studies of African Americans during these decades follow the two models, almost invariably focusing on one or the other population and suggesting distinctive patterns of social and political development. On the one side, there are African American communities of the free, albeit virulently racist, North that manage to construct their own institutions, publicly press their claims for full inclusion in American society, articulate a variety of aspirations for the future, and play key roles in the antislavery movement.[25] On the other side, there are African American communities of the slave South that engage in much more modest (and for the most part clandestine) efforts at institution building, that struggle to protect themselves from the worst of slavery's exploitation and degradation and, as best as possible, to readjust the balances of power, and that may show enormous cultural creativity but have no recognized access to public arenas of discussion, debate, or contention.[26] Although there was a great deal of movement and communication between these populations and sets of communities, there has been remarkably little effort to examine the mutual influences that resulted. The Civil War and Reconstruction, then, have come to serve as moments of encounter or reacquaintance: in the Union Army, in federal contraband camps, in the Union-occupied South, in postwar freedmen's conventions, and in other forms of political organizing, as northern and southern blacks met one another at new sites.[27]

Yet, if the boundaries of slavery are recognized as being national rather than sectional in their dimensions, the landscape of African American politics and political culture may be reconfigured as well. It may be possible for us to imagine much larger circuits of communication and experience, much more interconnected processes of negotiation and agitation, much deeper wells of aspiration and practice. And it may make sense for us to consider the enclaves of African Americans in New England, the Middle Atlantic, and the Midwest not so much as "free black communities," but as entities that resembled "maroons," communities of fugitives from slavery lodged in a society in which slavery still lived.[28]

Marronage has not figured very significantly in scholarly perspectives on slave cultures and forms of slave resistance either in colonial North America or—especially—in the United States. If anything, it has served as a counterpoint to slave societies of the Caribbean and Brazil, where communities of runaway slaves developed early, could embrace populations numbering in the hundreds or thousands, might survive for decades or even centuries, and occasionally forced colonial regimes to seek peace with them and sign treaties that acknowledged the maroons' political integrity: where, in short, maroons helped shape the politics and deployments of power in slave societies.[29]

Maroon activity did erupt during the first two centuries of slavery in North America, especially among newly arrived Africans and in an arc stretching from the Carolinas south and west toward the lower Mis-

sissippi Valley. The presence of rival European colo-
nizing powers on the continent and of numerous Indian tribes and confederations in the interior created
the necessary political room for this; the vast expanse
of wooded, swampy, and mountainous terrain offered the necessary physical room. By the late seventeenth century Spanish Florida was already a haven
for fugitive slaves from South Carolina and Georgia
and already a headache for their British masters.
Runaways headed for settlements like Gracia Real de
Santa Teresa de Mose near St. Augustine or perhaps
looked for sanctuary among the Seminole Indians.
Then they not only acted as magnets for other dis-
contented slaves but also played roles in sparking the
Stono Rebellion in 1739, together with American military forays intent on crushing them. Elsewhere, maroons took hold in the swamps on the borders of
Florida and Georgia, of North Carolina and Virginia,
along the Savannah River, in the bayous of lower
Louisiana, and at various points in the foothills of
the Appalachians, sometimes in alliance with Indians.[30]

But the political room for marronage seems to
have narrowed after the Seven Years' War, and even
more so after the American Revolution and the War
of 1812. The French, British, and Spanish were forced

to retreat and shift their imperial ambitions to other fields. American slaveholders won their political independence and achieved significant, if not dominant, influence over state and national policy. The Indians were left to face land-hungry Americans intent on pushing them west without the benefit of European allies. And the interior districts east of the Mississippi River began to fill with thousands of hostile white settlers. Maroons did hold on in highly inaccessible areas such as the Great Dismal Swamp, and "gangs" or "bands" of slaves and free blacks were occasionally reported to be congregating in swampy or forested enclaves from the Carolinas and Georgia to Alabama, Mississippi, Louisiana, and Texas and creating a local nuisance. But the rapid plantation development of the Deep South in the 1820s and 1830s and the two Seminole Wars in Florida appear to have kept maroons in check and to have effectively destroyed their political influence.[31]

Or so it seems. Perspectives on marronage, like perspectives on slave rebellions more generally, have for the most part been informed by rather limited and one-dimensional images and understandings of what a maroon is. Most tend to grow out of readings of the classic accounts of maroons in seventeenth-century Brazil (such as Palmares), or in eighteenth-century Jamaica and Surinam. These were usually large-scale settlements of runaway slaves, chiefly in remote areas, that were African in their demographic and cultural orientations and marked by tight political and military organization. They either preyed on plantations within reach or sought to become relatively self-sufficient, and they commanded the attention of public officials as well as local slave owners, sometimes from positions of strength. The historian Eugene D. Genovese regards their political impulse as being "restorationist," insofar as they endeavored to re-create the relations and hierarchies of the African worlds from which most of them came. In these respects, there is relatively little in either colonial North America or the nineteenth-century United States—outside Florida—that can compare.[32]

But, in truth, marronage in the Americas suggests a much more dynamic, and historically contingent, phenomenon. Considered as groups or collections of fugitives seeking some sort of existence outside enslavement, maroons took on many different guises and changed steadily over time and space. In general, they were more likely to be small and to be found in relatively close proximity to towns and plantations, especially if the slave society lacked difficult terrain or was dominated chiefly by plantation agriculture.

And, in general, they were important sites of cultural and political development. But although early maroons tended to be heavily African, even if ethnically diverse, by the late eighteenth and nineteenth centuries they could be increasingly Creole and show the many marks of the plantation cultures from which their inhabitants came. The most substantial of them might succeed in extracting concessions and official standing from the local slaveholding regime, though only after years of intense warfare and only at the price of contributing to the political stability of slavery. More commonly, they were perpetually harassed, lived in parasitic relation with slave plantations and farms, survived for short periods, and took some part—on occasion a leading part—in the slave rebellions that occurred. In their political organization and sensibilities, maroons could reflect, even by means of inversion or parody, the prevailing colonial or local power. In the Caribbean, they could be maritime in nature; fugitives headed by sea to islands at the "frontiers" of settlement or, once emancipation commenced, to islands where slavery had already been abolished.[33]

These more complex—and more culturally and politically located—representations of maroons confound neat analytical categories such as "restorationist" and open up a range of interpretive possibilities for regarding them as political formations. And they offer good reason for considering numerous settlements of people of African descent in what we have come to call the American North as historically specific variants of the broad phenomenon of maroons, especially in the period after the emancipation process had begun and perhaps increasingly as the antebellum era wore on. Indeed, an interesting case can be made for marronage in terms of the demographics, patterns of migration and residency, social and cultural formations, and political organizations to be found in them.

We still know relatively little about African American settlements in the northern states before the Civil War, particularly those outside major cities, and it would be impossible to determine just how many of those African Americans, at any point, were fugitives from slavery. But there are clues, and they are intriguing. The federal census shows that by 1850 substantial portions of the black populations of northern cities had been born in the slave states of the South. The proportions ranged from just under 25 percent in Boston, Providence, Brooklyn, and New York City, to about 50 percent in Philadelphia and Pittsburgh, to nearly 60 percent in Buffalo (across the border from Canada), to almost 75 percent in Cincinnati (perched on the northern bank of the Ohio River), to as high as 90 percent in the rural hinterlands of southern Ohio. And those proportions generally increased during the 1850s. One study that sampled the black inhabitants of Boston, Buffalo, Chicago, Cincinnati, and Detroit between 1850 and 1860 found that around two-thirds of them were southern-born. To these may be added both the children of southern migrants (or fugitives) as well as those who had recently been slaves in these cities and states and had endured gradual emancipation. Which is to say that African Americans who had directly experienced slavery and had escaped it either by flight or by manumission of some sort composed the majority of blacks throughout the North during this period.[34]

Black settlements in the antebellum North often came to resemble maroons not simply because they included substantial numbers of fugitives but also because of the ways in which they developed in relation to the larger world of slavery around them. Although African Americans by no means lived in segregated enclaves or, as some urban historians might term it, in precursors to ghettoes (slavery's marks of "integration" continued in evidence), their residential patterns increasingly showed what can be described as clusterings: groups of households and families living in close proximity that could range in size from relatively few to scores. The clusterings, moreover, were ordinarily concentrated in the poorer, working-class sections of towns or cities, if not wholly on their outskirts; and in the rural areas, where populations were more scattered and blacks might live in "associative settlements" (a form of clustering), the social separation could be even more pronounced.[35]

These residential clusterings, whether in urban or rural settings, were important because they served as the basis of social networks, of vital communication that linked blacks not only across the face of northern towns and rural districts but also to those who remained in slavery either nearby or at a distance. Like maroons, the clusterings thereby became beacons for slaves contemplating flight and refuges for those who ultimately made their escape. There is, of course, a trope familiar to antislavery literature—sometimes found in the narratives of runaways themselves—that depicts the north side of the Ohio River or Mason-Dixon line as the general destination of slaves who sought freedom, reached through a combination of cleverness, perseverance, courage, and abolitionist assistance. And there is truth in this. But fugitives more commonly headed to particular locations made known to them by family and friends who may have gone before or by the information that circulated between communities of slaves and those of freed blacks and fugitives. Cities, towns, and rural enclaves of the lower Midwest attracted runaways chiefly from Kentucky and western Virginia, and to a lesser extent from Tennessee, Georgia, and Mississippi; those of the Northeast and Middle Atlantic drew them from Maryland, Delaware, and eastern Virginia, and to a lesser extent from the Carolinas. During the last thirty years of the antebellum era, more than five thousand African Americans, a good many of them fugitives, arrived at sites in southeastern Pennsylvania (such as in Lancaster County), often having crossed over from farms and plantations in neighboring Maryland.[36]

Like maroons, these enclaves of fugitives and freed blacks across the northern states gave rise to their own leaderships, social structures, institutions, and cultural practices. In the larger cities they might develop around—or in some relation to—family networks of African Americans who had been free, become educated, and accumulated property and who might fashion an agenda for collective struggle that combined support for the enslaved in the South and North with notions of civil and political respectability familiar to an emerging white middle class. Their social hierarchies would, accordingly, be multitiered and complex. In towns and rural areas, on the other hand, the enclaves might develop around early or sponsored groups of fugitives—such as those aided by the Quakers in Indiana or New Jersey—or around communities of freeborn or manumitted blacks who had skills, literacy, and some property, who might seek to be self-sustaining, and who might prefer distance from rather than inclusion in the dominant white society. Their social hierarchies would be less easily marked, their top and bottom rungs in closer embrace. Everywhere black settlements and enclaves developed around churches and benevolent societies of their own making and around political calendars of their own design, which, among other things, commemorated signal events of an unfolding emancipation process: the abolition of the international slave trade, the ending of slavery in their particular states, and the abolition of slavery in the British West Indies. Everywhere, too, their inhabitants fought among themselves, sometimes bitterly, over how best to define and pursue their aspirations and sensibilities.[37]

Perhaps most significantly, the northern settlements and enclaves of fugitives and freed blacks—like maroons—everywhere shared a fundamental political orientation to the world around them. They were "under siege." And what organized that besieging world was not just racism, not just codes of racial discrimination, subordination, and exclusion, not just tempers of hostility and hatred. What organized that world was slavery. Whether in cities, towns, or rural districts, these black settlements were the anomalies in a nation in which people of African descent were presumed to be slaves and in which the claims of slaveholders were generally conceded by courts and legislatures. "It is a very prevalent error that there are no slaves in this state," a committee of New York blacks could charge in 1837 (a decade after the state declared slavery officially dead), citing the "common practice" of "persons having estates in the South, who reside here, [to] keep slaves" and then "remove them after a residence of several years, to the South, and dispose of these as slaves in the markets." "I hold it as a just construction of the law," the fictionalized northern Judge Ballard proclaims in Martin Delany's novel, *Blake*, "that not only has the slaveholder the right to reclaim his slave when and wherever found, but by its provision every free black in the country,

34

CAUTION!!

COLORED PEOPLE

OF BOSTON, ONE & ALL,

You are hereby respectfully CAUTIONED and advised, to avoid conversing with the

Watchmen and Police Officers of Boston,

For since the recent ORDER OF THE MAYOR & ALDERMEN, they are empowered to act as

KIDNAPPERS

AND

Slave Catchers,

And they have already been actually employed in KIDNAPPING, CATCHING, AND KEEPING SLAVES. Therefore, if you value your LIBERTY, and the *Welfare of the Fugitives* among you, *Shun* them in every possible manner, as so many *HOUNDS* on the track of the most unfortunate of your race.

Keep a Sharp Look Out for KIDNAPPERS, and have TOP EYE open.

APRIL 24, 1851.

THEODORE PARKER'S PLACARD

Placard written by Theodore Parker and printed and posted by the Vigilance Committee of Boston after the rendition of Thomas Sims to slavery in April, 1851.

Warning posted by the Boston Vigilance Committee after the passage of the 1850 Fugitive Slave Law.

Courtesy of the American Antiquarian Society, Worcester, Massachusetts.

North and South, are liable to enslavement by any white person." "They are," Ballard pronounced, "free men by suffrance or slaves-at-large."[38]

The black settlements were, therefore, subject to regular invasion by slave catchers seeking to kidnap their members or by white mobs looking to destroy or drive them out. In neither case did the invaders observe a distinction between African Americans who were fugitives and those who were legally free, and in both cases, they usually acted with the sanction or support of white authorities—of police officers, sheriffs, aldermen, judges, and lawyers—especially after Congress toughened the Fugitive Slave Law in 1850. As a consequence, northern blacks lived in constant fear, whatever their legal status, and, like maroons in the southern states or in other parts of the hemisphere, they and their communities had to be perpetually alert, perpetually on guard, perpetually self-protective. "After a few years of life in a Free State," William Parker, who fled from Maryland to the rural hinterlands of Philadelphia, later recalled, "I found by bitter experience that to preserve my stolen liberty I must pay, unremittingly, an almost sleepless vigilance."[39]

Organized self-defense was crucial. By the mid-1830s vigilance committees had been established by

African Americans in the major cities of the East Coast, taking as their responsibility the harboring of fugitive slaves as well as the thwarting of "slave agents and kidnappers." To those ends, they monitored waterfronts for the arrival of runaways or of vessels suspected as "slavers." They reported on the arrests and abductions of blacks purported to be fugitives, and on the whereabouts of slave catchers. And they made efforts to recover blacks who had been carried back into the South. When Frederick Douglass made his escape from Baltimore to New York City in 1838, he was quickly put in touch with David Ruggles, leader of the New York Vigilance Committee. Ruggles promptly hid Douglass, helped reunite Douglass with his wife, and, upon learning of Douglass's skills as a caulker, directed him to New Bedford, Massachusetts, where Douglass could find work and a community of African Americans.[40]

The circulation of information was therefore central to black self-defense. But so was direct resistance, some of it armed. The vigilance committees did more than spirit fugitives to relative safety in the very dangerous environments of the North, where, as one put it, proslavery sentiments "pervade[d]." They did more than alert vulnerable blacks to kidnappers who might be lurking. They also mobilized black members and community supporters to rescue blacks from abduction and physically drive off those who threatened. In these endeavors, the vigilance committees, generally headed by African Americans with skills and means, were aided by less formal groups of poor, working-class blacks, who utilized their own networks based in clustered households and work sites.

Thus, self-defense in these black enclaves involved, as it did in maroons, not only organization and communication but also fierce confrontations. Consider the episode that has come to be known as the Christiana Riot. In the late summer of 1851, a Maryland slaveholder named Edward Gorsuch set out to capture four of his slaves who had run off two years before and were rumored to be in Lancaster County, Pennsylvania. Gorsuch first headed by train to Philadelphia, where he obtained warrants under the auspices of the Fugitive Slave Law of 1850. With the help of a federal commissioner there, he also received the assistance of a deputy United States marshal and two local policemen, who made up, together with his own party from Maryland, very much a militarized posse. They then left for Lancaster County, having split into four groups to avoid detection.

Their concerns about detection suggest that the

Fugitive slaves and their allies battling slaveholders and slave catchers who carried federal warrants in Christiana, Pennsylvania, 1851.

From William Still, *The Underground Railroad* (Philadelphia, 1872), 351.

Gorsuch posse expected trouble. In fact, the trouble was already brewing. A black Philadelphia tavern keeper and member of a "special secret committee," Samuel Williams, had apparently learned of the warrants issued to Gorsuch, and he himself headed to Lancaster County to warn black inhabitants and fugitives of what was afoot. He knew whom to find and where to find them. African Americans in and around the village of Christiana, led by the fugitive William Parker, had years earlier formed "an organization for mutual protection against slaveholders and kidnappers and had resolved to prevent any of our brethren being taken back into slavery." They could pass intelligence with great speed and, with the sound of a horn, summon large numbers of local blacks to come to their aid. By the time the Gorsuch posse arrived in Christiana and began to move on William Parker's house, somewhere between 75 and 150 black men and women, armed with an assortment of pistols, rifles, scythes, corn cutters, and other farm tools, were making their way there, too. In the ensuing clash, Edward Gorsuch was shot dead (perhaps by one of his former slaves) and his son was badly wounded. For their part, Parker and two of the fugitives quickly fled north, to Toronto by way of Rochester, New York, where they were helped by a former Maryland acquaintance of Parker's, Frederick Douglass.[41]

Viewed from the perspective of the early twenty-first century, the Christiana Riot may be seen as a version of the many "race riots" that have plagued the history of the United States, just as enclaves and settlements of African Americans in urban areas may be studied in connection with the later phenomenon of racial and ethnic ghettoes. Yet, viewed from the perspective of the eighteenth and early nineteenth centuries, what happened in Christiana may perhaps better be understood as an example of paramilitary assaults on maroons that were endemic to the social and political history of slave societies in the Americas, and that had many (though lesser known) counterparts in the United States, North and South. William Parker, it should be noted, initially organized his mutual protection association during the 1830s—roughly two decades before the Christiana Riot—to combat the terrorist raids of local white toughs who organized as the Gap Gang, as well as the intermittent incursions of slave catchers. Although it would be a mistake to see the explosive riots that took place in New York, Boston, Philadelphia, and Cincinnati during the 1830s as the main examples of violent invasions of fugitive and freed black settlements, it might be useful to look at them, like the Christiana episode, through the lens of paramilitarism.[42]

The invasions were in fact many, though often small in scale, and they formed part of the complex political history of these settlements. On the one hand, the settlements always and everywhere occupied unstable political ground owing to the origins of their populations, the gradual and in many ways incomplete nature of the emancipation process, and the commitment of the federal government to protecting the property rights of slaveholders. Fugitive slaves commonly found themselves moving from one place to another in search of some semblance of safety and security, only to recognize that they had to leave the territory of the United States. In the lower Midwest the political ground of the settlements was particularly unstable owing to the black codes passed by state legislatures there.[43]

At the same time, the fugitive and freed black settlements had white allies—a sympathetic white man named Castner Hanway, a neighbor of William Parker's who tried to defuse the threat, was subsequently tried for treason—and in the federal political system of the United States, those alliances could carry consequence. The personal liberty laws enacted by numerous northern states as a response to the Fugitive Slave Laws testified to a distinctive political culture—one quite different from the colonial regimes that maroons elsewhere in the Americas encountered—as well as to an emancipation process that had begun to unfold. Even so, we must not forget that the fugitive settlements were, and would remain, renegade

social and political entities that struggled for years
against invaders, many of whom had official sanction, if not official status, before their members were
lent some civil and political standing, and entitled to
counsel, to writs of habeas corpus, and to jury trials,
and their enemies subject to heavy penalties for kidnapping. All the while, African Americans in these
settlements did the hard work of developing and sus-
taining radical abolitionism. They subscribed to antislavery newspapers, organized their own societies,
carried out rescues, signed petitions, and conducted
debates about tactics, strategies, and suitable alliances. And, in their ability to attract and protect a
continuous flow of runaways from slavery, even in
the face of widespread public hostility, they kept the
emancipation process alive and deepened the crisis of
the Union.[44]

The maroon analogy, therefore, puts African
Americans even more squarely at the center of the abolitionist movement. But it also helps us to see fugitive and freed black settlements as important political meeting grounds and as sites for the construction
of new black politics. Here, in an almost unprecedented way, people of African descent who had experienced slavery as well as putative freedom, who had
lived in the South as well as the North, in the West

Indies and other parts of the Americas, in rural and urban environments, could encounter one another, share perspectives, exchange ideas, and begin to fashion political languages and political cultures that did not fit easily or readily into mainstream categories. Although we have learned more and more about relatively small numbers of articulate black leaders in these settlements who, in various ways, mixed proto-nationalism and respectability with claims to equality, we know far less about the overwhelming mass of black inhabitants who were laborers and domestics, often on the move, and prone to distinctive forms of militancy and public politics. It was a veritable kaleidoscope of cultural and political activity. Not until the contraband camps and black army units of the Civil War years would the country see anything like this range of African American political expression or anything like the social and cultural diversity that these sites embraced.[45]

The maroon analogy also enables us to think even more expansively about the slave politics and forms of political consciousness that developed and circulated in those areas of the country where slaves were concentrated, and how they intersected with black settlements in those areas of the country where most slaves were fugitives. The lives, thoughts, and activities of David Walker and Martin Delany may offer particularly compelling illustration of this process. Walker was born free in North Carolina in the mid-1790s and spent most of his life in the South, chiefly in the Carolinas, where he obviously obtained a substantial education and mingled with slaves and free people of color (including those in Denmark Vesey's Charleston), before ending up in Boston in the late 1820s. There he joined the African Lodge and the Massachusetts General Colored Association, became involved in antislavery activity, and served as an agent for *Freedom's Journal,* the first American newspaper published by African Americans. In 1829, shortly before his death, Walker published his fiery *Appeal to the Coloured Citizens of the World.* It was a tract remarkable not only for its angry eloquence and verbal power, but also for the ways in which it reflected intellectual and political currents flowing among African Americans, North and South, since the mid-eighteenth century: democratic-republicanism, millennialism, protonationalism, Pan-Africanism. His recent biographer thus regards Walker's life as an important chapter in the history of "antebellum slave resistance."[46]

Like Walker, Martin Delany was born of a free black mother and an enslaved father in a slave state (Virginia, in this case), though unlike Walker's, Delany's family relocated northward when he was still a child—to Chambersburg, Pennsylvania, not very far from Christiana. Moving on to Pittsburgh in 1831 at the age of nineteen, Delany obtained an education and immersed himself in newspaper editing, moral reform, and antislavery. He eventually attended medical school and spent time in Canada and West Africa. Delany's emerging black nationalism and interest in emigration are well known; less well known is his novel, *Blake; or, The Huts of America,* published in serial form in the late 1850s and early 1860s, in which the main character (variously Henrico Blacus, Henry Holland, and Blake), having been spirited away from the West Indies and sold into slavery in the Deep South, and having seen his wife sold off to Cuba, escapes and sets out to stir up a massive slave rebellion. Delany has his protagonist (at this point in the story, Henry) move quietly across the rural and urban South, from Louisiana and Texas, to Georgia and the Carolinas, to Tennessee and Kentucky, divulging his "scheme" for a "general insurrection of the slaves in every state, and the successful overthrow of slavery." Everywhere Henry goes, the slaves seem to be waiting for him, eagerly, and to have heard about his travels and plans, evidence of their own communication networks. He then returns to his plantation, leads other slaves to freedom in Canada, and finally heads to Cuba, where he rejoins his wife and becomes Blake, general in chief of an "army of emancipation."[47]

Delany's narrative may seem far-fetched and very much removed from the world of southern slavery. Then again, perhaps not. Delany journeyed through Louisiana, Texas, and Arkansas in 1839–40, and he was familiar with fugitive slave narratives, including those of Henry Bibb and Solomon Northup, from which he appears to have drawn. He surely was familiar with the experiences described by fugitives when they arrived in black settlements clustered in towns like Pittsburgh, and then circulated among local blacks and in the abolitionist press. But the riveting memoir of William Webb (published in 1873), who was a slave in Kentucky and Mississippi, gives us special reason to pay heed to the portrait of slave political life that Delany sketched in *Blake*.

Webb remembered that when John C. Frémont ran for president in 1856, the slaves first learned "about another nation wishing them to be free . . . and they understood the name Fremont meant freedom to them." "[T]hey held great meetings," he continued, "and had speeches among themselves, in secret . . . [putting] all their trust in Fremont to deliver them from bondage." Thus, "when Fremont ran and was defeated . . . the slaves began to study how they would get free, and they held [more] meetings and . . . would make speeches . . . to the best of their knowledge about what steps to take. Some would speak about rebelling and killing, and some would speak, and say, 'wait for another four years' . . . [feeling] as if the next president would set the colored people free."[48]

Webb went on to describe complex lines of communication, stretching over many hundreds of miles, that transmitted various forms of intelligence and served as the basis for widespread organizing among the slaves. That Webb also presented himself as one of the main organizers might raise serious questions about his own veracity were it not that so much other—albeit often fragmentary—evidence lends credibility to his claims. This evidence suggests that ideas, information, and rumors moved north to south and around the South, as well as south to north, enabling slaves to learn about the larger political terrain of the times, about the fugitive settlements where semblances of freedom were to be had, about allies, white and black, who spoke and mobilized against slavery, and about the struggles of slaves erupting beyond the borders of the United States. Slaves learned these things from different sources in different ways: from white politicians they overheard during court days and campaigns, from newspapers and smuggled tracts (such as Walker's *Appeal*) that could be read by the handful of them who were literate, from migrants and refugees from the Caribbean who arrived in Charleston, Savannah, Pensacola, Mobile, and New Orleans, from slaveholders who expressed their fears and concerns within earshot, and from fugitives who returned to ferry more slaves to black settlements in the North. Most often, they learned from each other: from slaves who had mobility, who worked in the Big House, who were hired out in towns and on docks, who were coachmen, boatmen, and tradesmen, and who then brought news back to their communities. In the process, slaves—in complex association with fugitives and freed blacks—constructed what might be called their own political narratives and discourses of expectation. The consequences would be enormous.[49]

☙

It may be thought that a reconsideration of the emancipation process in the United States that insists on linking the first and second emancipations and that challenges the sectional conflict interpretation of the antebellum era risks diminishing the significance of the Civil War and of the massive emancipation that occurred in its midst. But this could not be further from the case. Indeed, by suggesting that slavery must be regarded as a national rather than sectional institution, that emancipation proceeded slowly and incompletely where it commenced, that maroons may have been widespread and politically consequential within the territorial limits of the country, and that the political dynamics of the period were international and involved a large cast of actors, including slaves and freed people, the Civil War and the emancipation it made possible become even more significant, even more stunning events of truly world-historical importance.

Why is this so? The early emancipation statutes remind us that gradualism was the predominant way in which slavery was abolished most everywhere in the Americas, and that so long as the social and political power of slaveholders remained intact, the road from slavery to freedom would be not only long but so delimited by the invention and adoption of new coercive mechanisms (enforced by the state) that freedom itself would be little more than a rhetorical fiction. Without the Civil War, or with a war that ended differently—including by armistice, a more than possible outcome—emancipation would eventually have continued but in such a protracted fashion and with such encumbrances that the United States would have had slaves into the twentieth century, together with a large ex-slave population officially relegated to subordinate status and possessing few if any rights of citizenship. In short, it would have been a world the Supreme Court's *Dred Scott* decision framed. Like the Haitian Revolution before it, the Civil War broke the logic of gradualism and slaveholder compensation and made a new and different country.[50]

By regarding slavery as a national institution, we are also reminded of the immense challenges that emancipation confronted and of the many struggles required to force a showdown over it. If slavery was not simply "southern," people throughout the nation had either a substantial investment in it or limited scruples against it; and if sectionalism no longer serves as the chief axis of analysis, there was little "irrepressible," in social or economic terms, about the battle over slavery. Politics thereby assumes primacy, and the universe of political activity and contest becomes far larger than customarily imagined, encompassing much of the Western Hemisphere and both sides of the Atlantic.

By recognizing slavery as a national institution and the appeal of gradualism even to a great many northerners who moved into the antislavery camp, there is also a deeper sense both of the revolutionary meaning of Civil War-era emancipation and of the profound limits to how far that revolution could go. Sectionalism, long considered the centerpiece of American development during the first half of the nineteenth century, may come to be seen less as a "fact" or as a "reflection" of an assortment of social forces, and more as an immensely important political construction—as much a project of incipient state building as of popular mobilizations around questions of slavery and freedom. Owing to the critiques of abolitionists, antislavery partisans, and social reformers during the antebellum decades, and later of government officials, scientific experts, and other intellectuals, the South would be represented as the backward, benighted, and retrograde section of the country, as a serious "problem" for the nation's future, and very much in need of treatment, healing, and rejuvenation by the federal government.[51]

If we come to regard emancipation as a protracted national process, we must also take a new look at the dimensions of what we call Reconstruction. Either Reconstruction must be seen as a similarly extended phenomenon, initiated in the northern states well before the southern (and thus almost coincidental with American nation building more generally), or we have to acknowledge a great many more "rehearsals" for the large-scale Reconstruction of the Civil War era: rehearsals that suggest different and more wide-ranging political dynamics (involving class, ethnicity, gender, and culture as much as race) than we are accustomed to recognizing.[52] At all events, we may appreciate more fully the role that African Americans and women's rights activists played, through their northern mobilizations of the 1830s and 1840s, in setting Reconstruction's agenda for debate, just as we may take even more sobering account of the obstacles to change in the United States. The question, that is, may no longer be "Why did Reconstruction fail?" but, rather, "What did the achievements and limitations of Reconstruction together signify?" Viewing emancipation as a process, and as a protracted one, quite simply recasts our perspective on a major and formative era of American history.

2

Did We Miss the Greatest Slave Rebellion in Modern History?

In the late summer of 1862, slaveholders residing along the coast of Georgia complained bitterly to Confederate officials about the behavior of their slaves. The slaves, it seems, were fleeing their plantations in large numbers, heading for Union lines, joining up with the Union Army, and then returning to the plantations to entice still more slaves away. The slaveholders thus demanded "a few executions of the leading transgressors . . . by hanging or shooting," which they regarded as "punishment adequate to their crime."

Nearly four months later, when the complaints finally reached the desk of Confederate Secretary of War James A. Seddon, it became clear what "crime" the slaves had committed. "The question as to the Slaves taken in federal Uniform and with arms in their hands has been considered on conference with the President," Seddon reported. "Slaves in flagrant rebellion are subject to death by the laws of every slave holding State. They cannot be recognized in any way as soldiers subject to the rules of war and to trial by Military Courts, [for] slaves in armed insurrection should meet condign punishment. [S]ummary execution must therefore be inflicted on those taken, as with the slaves referred [to by the Georgia slaveholders], under circumstances indicative beyond doubt of actual rebellion."[1]

It may not surprise us to learn that slaveholders and their political representatives would consider their slaves' flight to, and then alliance with, the Union Army as "rebellious" and "insurrectionary," as "indicative of actual rebellion." Much lesser activities on the part of slaves provoked their masters to a state of alarm, if not of apoplexy, before the war; and once hostilities commenced, the correspondence and diaries of slaveholding southerners and Confederates describing the doings of slaves crackled with language of rebellion and revolt. They spoke of "disturbances," "contagions," "symptoms of revolt," "terrible stirs," "stampedes," "mutinies," "intentions to spring," "strikes," "turn outs," and "states of insurrection." The Reverend Charles Colcock Jones, evangelist to the slaves and onetime reformer, was surely not confused about how to regard "Negro slaves absconding to the enemy." "Can such Negroes be summarily dealt with under any acts of the state?" he asked. "Could they be taken up under the head of insurrection? Could their overt rebellion in the way of casting off the authority of their masters be made by construction insurrection?"[2]

What seemed so obvious to slaveholders and Confederate officials at the time, however, has been widely resisted or rejected by historians. This despite the roughly half a million slaves who, by war's end, had fled to Union lines and the nearly 150,000 who took up arms for the Union. Indeed, whatever their disagreements on other matters—and those are many—historians of the Civil War and emancipation, with the possible exception of W. E. B. Du Bois, almost universally share the view that, despite contemporary fears to the contrary, the war did not precipitate a slave rebellion, that whatever the slaves did in pursuit of their freedom is not to be regarded as rebellion. Even the late Herbert Aptheker, who identified far more rebellious and insurrectionary activity among American slaves than any other historian, did not believe that a major rebellion erupted during the Civil War itself. "Concrete instances of conspiracy or revolt come from practically all of the slave states," he wrote of the war years, but these were small in scale; he went on to call a plot hatched near Troy, Alabama, in late 1864 "the last slave conspiracy within the present borders of the United States." Tellingly, Aptheker's chapter on the Civil War is by far the shortest in his best-known work, *American Negro Slave Revolts.*[3]

Why is it that historians—even those interested in the slaves' "agency" and in their forms of "resistance" to enslavement—have been so reluctant to entertain seriously the idea that the Civil War may have witnessed a massive rebellion of southern slaves? The answer, perhaps, has less to do with the plausibility of such an interpretation than with the politics of history writing and memory making and with the challenges of imagining slaves as political actors.

The case for slave rebellion does not have to be dug up, teased out, or deconstructed. It is neither hidden, archivally silenced, nor subtly discursive. Quite simply, it stares us in the face. And although the case is by no means indisputable, the documentation that has been compiled over the years lends it a great deal of support, if that evidence does not lead us right up to its embrace.

Slave rebellion was, of course, the "great fear" haunting both sides in the Civil War. Confederates obviously worried that full-scale troop mobilizations

would undermine the customary methods of polic-
ing on the home front and encourage the slaves to
rise. So concerned were they that policy makers took
steps to bolster security (the Twenty Negro Law, which
exempted from military service owners or overseers
of plantations with twenty or more slaves, being the
most notorious example) that simultaneously exacer-
bated social tensions among whites by favoring slaveholders at the expense of nonslaveholders. But Union
authorities were troubled as well both because they
initially pledged to leave the South's "established institutions" undisturbed and because slave unrest would
vastly complicate their goal of crushing the Confederate rebellion militarily. Thus, when in April 1861
General Benjamin F. Butler marched his Massachusetts troops south toward Fortress Monroe, Virginia,
he offered to "co-operate" with Governor Thomas
Hicks of Maryland in "suppressing" any slave "insurrection" that might break out. Other Union officials
ordered their officers and troops on the ground elsewhere to do the same and made the orders publicly
known.[4]

The federal perspective on "negro insurrection"
and slave unrest more generally was not only a product of military expediency; it also reflected early
Union policy on slavery and emancipation. This was

to be a white man's war over the future of the country, and as far as possible "the rights and property" of the white southern people were to be respected to "strengthen the Union sentiment."[5] Yet such respect was easier to proclaim than enforce, and before the ink was dry, federal policy was in disarray.

The disarray, as scholars now generally agree, was produced by the slaves themselves, acting in ways that neither side had adequately anticipated. The slaves disrupted both the workings of plantations and farms on the Confederate home front and the operations of Union Army camps on the battlefront. Slowly but steadily, they forced federal policy makers to reassess their status in the developing war effort and as recruits to the Union military. By 1863 Lincoln had come to accept uncompensated emancipation and black enlistment (and had jettisoned colonization), and it would be difficult to find a reputable historian these days who does not think that the slaves had a significant role in bringing their emancipation about. The question is how to interpret that role—how to interpret what the slaves did—in political terms.

Our understanding of what the slaves did during the Civil War generally commences with their response to the Union invasion of the Confederate

South in the spring and summer of 1861, and more specifically with their flight from plantations and farms to Union lines. They made their initial appearance at Fortress Monroe in southeastern Virginia, arriving as individuals or in small groups, overwhelmingly young and male, and by the time of the first Battle of Bull Run (in mid-July), they numbered nearly one thousand. The volume and character of slaves' flight then changed rather dramatically when the northern armies moved into the densely populated plantation districts of coastal South Carolina (November 1861) and the lower Mississippi Valley (spring 1862). Now the slaves came, not chiefly as individuals or in small "squads," but as larger groups, often linked by kinship, encompassing much of the labor force of entire plantations and farms. A chaplain under General Ulysses S. Grant's command could therefore marvel at the "vast numbers" of blacks who flocked to "the camps of the Yankees." It was, he gasped, "like the coming of cities."[6]

By the middle of 1864 nearly 400,000 slaves had made their way to Union lines. Their numbers were greatest in the border South and the Mississippi Valley states where northern armies had long been conducting operations, and, to a lesser extent, along the Atlantic Coast, where small federal outposts had for

Slaves, having fled from their owners, arriving at a Union Army encampment in North Carolina.

Harper's Weekly, 21 February, 1863, 116.

some time been attracting fugitives. Although precise figures are impossible to obtain, a reasonable estimate of those behind the lines would be between one-tenth and one-quarter of the slave populations of Tennessee, Missouri, Kentucky, Arkansas, Mississippi, Virginia, and the Carolinas. But the significance of this phenomenon was not simply in its scale; it was also in the dynamic of social and political change set in motion.[7]

The slaves' departures from the plantations and farms both challenged the will and authority of their owners and forced the Union side to tamper with the institution (slavery) it had originally vowed to respect. The Union had to figure out what to do with the fugitive slaves, especially once it became clear that the Confederates were impressing slaves to work at their own military sites—in effect, using slaves to aid their rebellion. Union officials began by declaring the fugitive slaves to be "contrabands of war" and putting them to work on Union fortifications. As the ranks of the fugitives continued to swell, officials began to establish "contraband camps" at various points in the Upper and Lower South, which then acted as magnets for many other slaves contemplating flight and, in some cases, grew to sizes that dwarfed even the largest plantations to be found in the antebellum South. Before too long, the slaves' flight opened up the question of emancipation as a war measure and a way of weakening the Confederacy. By the summer of 1862, in the Second Confiscation Act, the U.S. Congress declared that all slaves owned by Confederate masters would be free once they crossed into Union lines.[8]

At the same time, the war-induced flight of slaves began shifting the terrain of experience and struggle for those slaves who, owing to circumstance or choice, stayed put. On the Magnolia Plantation in Plaquemines Parish, Louisiana, slaves demanded pay for their work and engaged in a slowdown when the demand was rejected. Not long after, all the women at Magnolia went on strike and refused to return to the fields despite the urging of a federal army officer brought in to encourage cooperation. By the end of October, the only work the hands had completed presented the plantation managers with a chilling sight: they had erected gallows in the quarters, claiming to have been told that they "must drive the [managers] off the plantation" and "hang their master" before "they will be free." Elsewhere, slaves, less threateningly but no less effectively, renegotiated the relations and expectations of farm and plantation life. Their masters agreed to offer them small wages or shares of the crop and to allow them more control over operations on the estates in order to deter flight.[9]

The Civil War's increasingly revolutionary dynamic was perhaps best embodied by the Emancipation Proclamation, not only because it declared "all persons held as slaves" in the rebellious states "henceforth" free, but also because it provided for receiving "such persons of suitable condition . . . into the armed forces of the United States." There would be neither gradualism (as there had been in the northern states) nor any form of monetary compensation to slave owners (as there had been in Washington, D.C., and the British slave colonies). And a longstanding practice of American military life had been dramatically overturned. Since the ratification of the Constitution, African Americans, whether slave or free, had been excluded from the federal army and the state militias; given President Lincoln's initial war aims and the temper of public opinion, early efforts to contest this policy and win approval merely for the enrollment of northern blacks had met with swift rebuffs. Across the North, state and local officials and regimental commanders rejected offers of service tendered by black leaders and prospective recruits, and their actions were quickly sustained by the Lincoln administration. "This Department," Simon Cameron, Lincoln's secretary of war, bluntly asserted, "has no intention to call into the service of the Government any colored soldiers."[10]

Bolder initiatives undertaken by abolition-minded officers in the field—John C. Frémont, James H. Lane,

John W. Phelps, and David Hunter chief among them—to recruit slaves as soldiers met with a range of disapprobation (Frémont was dismissed from service). But a process had been initiated that, owing to a shortage of white Union manpower and an excess of male fugitives within Union lines, soon proved irresistible. In the late summer of 1862, the War Department, in a surprise move, authorized the establishment of a black regiment in coastal South Carolina, and by late fall the First South Carolina Volunteers, composed of former slaves under the command of the New England abolitionist Thomas Wentworth Higginson, had taken shape.[11]

Still, full-scale mobilization had to await the Emancipation Proclamation. Only then did the federal government permit northern governors to begin enrolling black men living in their states (a good many of whom were fugitive slaves or their children), and nearly three-quarters of all those between the ages of eighteen and forty-five (32,671) came forward: a much higher proportion than was true among eligible northern white men. By far the greatest number of black soldiers, however, came to be recruited in the slave states, and especially in the slave states of the Confederacy. Totaling 140,313, they constituted, by the last year of the war, well over 10 percent of the

Union Army, and in some departments close to half of it.[12]

Although federal officials initially imagined that black troops would serve as menial laborers behind the lines, thereby freeing up more white troops to do the fighting, within a very short time this neat distinction evaporated, and black troops, in substantial numbers, were to be found armed and in the heat of battle. And as any historian writing about their experience would be quick to acknowledge, black troops engaged in a forbidding and savage undertaking. They took up arms at a time of military stalemate, low morale in the North, and grave doubts among Union authorities about their potential military contributions. They were put to work doing degrading tasks in camp and occasionally sent into hopeless situations at the front, as many of their officers believed that black bodies were more expendable than white ones. Most threatening, they met an enemy—their former masters—who regarded them, as the coastal Georgia planters made plain, not as soldiers but as slaves in rebellion, and expected to treat them accordingly.

As Secretary of War Seddon's response to the complaint of the Georgia planters suggested, the slaves forced the Confederacy as well as the Union to concede that the fate of slavery was very much at the center of the war and, in so doing, tested the political meaning of their status. In late November 1862 President Jefferson Davis, already having conferred with Seddon, warned Confederate state governors that invading Union armies might provoke a "servile insurrection," and he soon thereafter ordered commanders to turn over "all negro slaves captured in arms . . . to the executive authorities of the respective States to which they belong to be dealt with according to the laws of said States": laws that invariably prescribed reenslavement or execution, usually by hanging. In the field, however, Confederate officers often chose to deal with the matter themselves. The most notorious episode came when General Nathan Bedford Forrest took Fort Pillow in Tennessee and had scores of black troops murdered after they surrendered (Forrest would later organize the Ku Klux Klan). But the murder of captured black soldiers on a smaller scale was widespread. "It was understood among us," one Confederate soldier wrote in 1864 from North Carolina, "that we take no negro prisoners." Blacks thereby fought with a special ferocity. As one northern observer reported, "there is death to the rebel in every black mans eyes."[13]

The Lincoln administration felt the need to act. As

early as the spring of 1863, the War Department provided black troops with belligerent status, required that they be regarded as public enemies rather than as felons and insurrectionists, and promised severe retaliation if they were enslaved and sold. Some months later, after reports of atrocities at Milliken's Bend, Battery Wagner, and Port Hudson provoked a storm of protest, Lincoln himself pledged to enforce the War Department's orders by having a rebel soldier executed or placed at hard labor for each violation. The murder and brutal treatment of black troops at the hands of Confederates did not cease—and there is no evidence that Lincoln ever moved to implement his pledge—but something of a juridical basis of equality was established in the ranks: a step along the crooked road leading away from the *Dred Scott* decision and toward the Fourteenth Amendment.[14]

As historians of the period would be quick to say or concede, the slaves played a crucial role in bringing about the unconditional surrender of the Confederacy and the uncompensated abolition of slavery, and they did so by violating, in the most blatant ways, the basic rules of slave plantation order. They fled from their plantations and farms in great numbers against the express commands of their own-

ers and often in the face of double-barreled shot-
guns or threats of reprisal against family and friends.
They served as scouts, guides, and spies for invading
Union armies, and they eventually took up arms in
the many thousands against their Confederate masters, allying themselves militarily and politically with
the United States government. Many of those who remained at "home" nonetheless contested the authority of their owners in ways that were central to the
meaning of enslavement: demanding pay, rejecting
close supervision, making decisions about life and labor themselves, coming and going as they pleased. In
some cases (perhaps in a good many more than we
have acknowledged), they took direct action against
their masters by sacking their estates and destroying
their property. Why shouldn't the slaveholders and
Confederates have seen rebellion and insurrection
percolating or being enacted at every turn?[15]

The historical record, it should be said, reveals relatively few examples (though perhaps more than we
might expect) of slaves wreaking vengeance through
personal violence or the torching of plantations or
farms. And this may be why historians are so reluctant to liken the slaves' wartime activities to a rebellion or set of rebellions. Authentic slave rebels, it
would seem, are supposed to do certain things. They

are supposed to conspire secretly, arm themselves, rise up, attempt to exterminate their oppressors, and try to find some means of either escaping slavery or overturning it. Alas, few such Civil War–era conspiracies and fewer, if any, such rebellions—even on a very limited basis—have ever been uncovered, even by those who were looking hard for them.[16]

Yet authentic, or model, slave rebels are exceptionally difficult to find anywhere, and the complex and varied practices and goals of slave rebellions reveal that political and historical contexts are always of signal importance in accounting for them. Some slave rebellions, including massive ones, began as acts of marronage or as efforts to bring about reform within the system of slavery. Some have had relatively delimited aims or, when erupting with explosive violence, have been quite selective in their targets. Some have shown spiritual and others chiefly secular inspirations, and many have demonstrated a mix of both. Most slave rebellions displayed political awareness that reached well beyond the confines of their localities and often imagined powerful allies either encouraging them or coming to their aid. Understood broadly as organized, and usually armed, resistance to established authority, rebellions—slave or any other—can, in short, take a great many forms, and we may especially have **underestimated** both the foundation-building activities and the political knowledge of slaves in the Civil War South.[17]

There is indeed an odd contradiction in most representations of the slaves' "response" to the Civil War. On the one hand, by beginning with the early, small-scale flight of slaves to Union lines, historians convey the impression either of spontaneous resistance to enslavement or of an equally spontaneous lifting of the veil of accommodation when opportunity arose; either way, there appears to have been no collective organization and very little political awareness. At the same time, historians generally account for the direction of the slaves' flight—to Union lines as opposed to the swamps, the hills, or the border— by the freedom slaves expected to find there: an assessment that clearly suggests some knowledge, understanding, or interpretation of the course of political events that slaves surely shared with one another. But the social and political implications of prior knowledge, understanding, or interpretation are rarely pursued. Why did some slaves, perhaps many slaves, believe that freedom beckoned behind Union lines? How did they come to think this? And what might it mean for our own perspectives on what the slaves were doing?

William Webb's arresting autobiography not only points to networks of communication and forums of organization that could extend over long distances, but also demonstrates that they could reverberate with political discussions, narratives, and discourses of expectation. Supporting evidence comes forth in a variety of forms, some in the accounts of slaves and former slaves such as Webb, some in testimonies presented at government hearings during the Civil War and Reconstruction, some in speeches commemorating emancipations or, perhaps, the independence of Liberia, and some in confessions rendered, often under duress, by those accused of plotting, abetting, or participating in acts of rebellion. More commonly, the evidence comes to us in fragments, in the papers and diaries of slaveholders or in reports printed in local newspapers, and thus in the words of white observers speculating on the causes of slave unrest.

Together, the evidence suggests that slaves could be acutely aware of conflicts that erupted between white people and nations ruled by white people; that slaves often imagined a set of possible allies and enemies; that slaves could be cognizant of the national and international struggle over slavery and the slave trade and, depending on where they resided, of momentous emancipations; that slaves often became conversant with institutions and issues of local and national politics and might develop sophisticated understandings of how the American political system operated; and that slaves fashioned interpretations of what seemed to be afoot, at times in ways that moved well beyond the intentions of the political actors. Signs of division or tension among white leaders, news of debates over policies related to slavery, hotly contested elections, especially presidential elections, even with no obvious connection to the slavery question—all could stir expectation. "The negroes," the Georgia politician and planter Howell Cobb could record during the national election of 1844, when the Liberty Party chose a presidential candidate, "are already saying to each other that great men are trying to set them free and will succeed."[18]

As the crisis over slavery deepened during the 1850s, hopes and expectations among slaves heightened, especially when the Republican Party made its first run at the presidency in 1856. By the fall of 1860, as the momentous presidential election of that year neared its conclusion, political expectations, discourses, and rumors flew widely. "During the campaign when Lincoln was first a candidate for the Presidency," Booker T. Washington, who grew up in western Virginia, later remembered, "the slaves on our far-off plantation, miles from any railroad or large city or daily newspaper, knew what the issues involved were," and "when the war was begun . . . every slave on our plantation felt and knew that, though other issues were discussed, the primal one was that of slavery." Indeed, evidence from all parts of the slave, and then Confederate, South suggests that a great many slaves knew of Lincoln, believed him to be their friend and ally (and the enemy of their owners), speculated that, once in power, he would move to free them, and saw the Union invasion of the Confederacy as a direct attack on slavery. Some went so far as to interpret Lincoln's inauguration as marking their own liberation: a liberation that would be enforced either when they rose to claim it or when Lincoln's soldiers arrived.[19]

Little is currently known, at least outside narratives like William Webb's, of meetings, discussions, and organizing among slaves between the fall of 1860 and the late spring of 1861. But what is known of the mechanisms of slave communication—patterns of mobility, hiring, literacy, spiritual practice, cultural transmission, the use of liminal terrain, in short, the construction and operation of what has long been called the grapevine telegraph—supplies clues as to how news and interpretation could have spread, and certainly puts the slaves' flight to Union lines in a much deeper and causal political context.

The slaves' response to the Union invasion of the Confederate South was not spontaneous, nor should it be regarded simply as a response to an event orchestrated from the outside. When the slaves fled their plantations and farms and headed to Union Army encampments, they instead acted on their understandings of the war's meaning, and given such unmistakable self-consciousness and the effective organizing that likely preceded their actions, the idea of a rebellion against the authority of their owners makes increasing sense. Thus, after the slave Harry Jarvis escaped a gun-toting master and sailed to Fortress Monroe sometime in the spring or early summer of 1861, he asked General Butler to let him enlist. Butler refused him, allowing that *"it wasn't a black man's war."* But Jarvis insisted otherwise, in turn explaining his very presence. "It *would* be a black man's war before they got through," he proclaimed.[20]

Jarvis not only made his way to Fortress Monroe by rejecting the authority of his master and by carrying clear ideas about what was going on and what he might find. He also relied heavily on the intelligence and support provided by slaves who had not yet decided to go: food while he hid out in the woods and particularly information about the reaction of his owner and the whereabouts of a boat. And Jarvis was by no means alone. Slaves who contemplated flight knew they would be assuming the status of runaways and rebels; and so they had to determine to their satisfaction the political stakes of the war, and they had to obtain more specific intelligence about the shifting of Union lines, the patrolling of Confederates or Home Guards, the location of enslaved allies, and the best trails to follow—which is to say that even small-scale flight was necessarily a collective undertaking.

But it was not simply acts of flight, informed by political interpretations and collective activities, that suggest a large and increasingly massive rebellion of slaves; it was also how the acts of flight made possible new forms of politicization and new forms of struggle against the institution of slavery. Indeed, while most recent historical accounts construct a narrative in which slaves are effectively assimilated to the nation, in which the goals of the slaves and those of the federal government steadily coincide, there is good reason to regard slaves—and slaves turned freed people—as discrete, ever-developing political and military bodies moving into and out of alliances as the circumstances of power and politics allowed.

The swelling number of slaves behind Union lines

who benefits from (not) having this perspective?

thus reflected a complex process that linked contrabands with slaves still on plantations and farms for
months, perhaps years, on end, while at the same
time creating new and expansive arenas of political
contact and discussion. When, for example, slaves
made it to Union lines, they presented themselves as
allies in what they thought to be a battle against slavery. Early on in the war, many Union officers rejected
such an alliance entirely by sending the slaves back
to their owners; eventually, by declaring them to be
"contrabands" and putting them to work on fortifications, the Union responded with its own version
of an alliance, one that left the slaves' freedom in
doubt and placed them in a subordinate position.
Most of the contrabands remained if they could, be-
lieving their circumstances superior and likely more
promising than what they would find back home.
Some thought otherwise and looked for other op-
tions. Harry Jarvis, who had reached Fortress Monroe as the contraband policy unfolded, was put to
work and claimed that he "was getting on well, till
one day I see a man given up to his master that come
for him." That was enough. Fortress Monroe, Jarvis
recalled, "was not the place for me," and he "hired on
to a ship going to Cuba, and then one a going to Africa." It was two years before he was ready again to of-

fer himself to the U.S. government as an ally. By that time "it had got to be a black man's war for sure," and Jarvis enlisted in the Fifty-fifth Massachusetts Infantry.

More generally, communications between contrabands and home plantations and farms continued, sometimes encouraging and sometimes discouraging slaves from taking flight. Relying on their own intelligence networks, slaves could learn whether fugitives might be denied entrance to Union Army posts, surrendered to demanding owners, impressed into military service, contracted to profit-hungry lessees, physically abused and sexually violated by Yankee soldiers, and generally treated with contempt. It was political acumen, not misplaced fidelity, that dissuaded the slave Moses, an elder and a community leader on a large Mississippi Valley plantation, from following the example of his "namesake of the Bible" and bringing his people "out of bondage." "They call me doubting Moses, and I have my own opinions," he told a Union Navy officer, citing the rough treatment meted out to "some of our bucks" who "run away and enlisted board a gun-boat." "If I had my way," Moses sighed, "I'd be on the Canada side: the colored man is safe there."[21]

The very process of arming the slaves—of incorporating them into the Union armed forces—revealed a thicket of political loyalties and alliances that had to be rearranged, negotiated, and, in some instances, coerced. The slaves, to be sure, widely relished the opportunity to help crush the Confederates and guarantee the end of slavery, at least where they were able to do so. In this sense, great numbers of them who had rebelled against their owners by means of flight chose to ally themselves with the Union militarily, thereby providing a powerful political center to the overall rebellion where experiences could be shared, goals debated, and leadership nurtured.

But it was not always that easy. Union Army recruiters might have to vie with loyal planters and northern lessees for access to able-bodied male laborers or, even more frequently, with the strong tugs of slave and freed kinship obligations. Some recruiters learned, when possible, to curry the favor and counsel of black community leaders who could call meetings, speak on the political issues of the war, and encourage the men to enlist. Others discovered that a major operation was required: setting up headquarters in a public building, house, or barn; sending small squads out to visit plantations and farms; and including black soldiers in the recruiting parties. At all events, success often demanded attention both to

Black Union soldiers, most former slaves, in a fierce fight with
Confederate troops in 1863.

Harper's Weekly, 14 March 1863, 168.

the concerns and sensibilities of potential recruits and to the needs and vulnerabilities of their families. Thus, after Union Army officers arrived at one plantation in St. Bernard Parish, Louisiana, in the late summer of 1863, they collected up the hands, "told them that now was the time to decide about being free or about being slaves for life," and explained "that they could take their families to N[ew] O[rleans] & they would be supported at Govt expense." One officer "then called up the women &c and made them a speech—Telling them that they were as free as himself . . . [and] might work as much or as little as they pleased." In the end, the officers "selected 71" men and managed to "t[ake] them off." When, however, persuasion failed and manpower needs outpaced the flow of black volunteers, the army could simply resort to impressment, occasionally staffing press gangs with black soldiers.[22]

The tensions between the political goals of black soldiers and the policies of the federal government were almost immediately in evidence and soon manifest on a number of fronts: in struggles over combat status, pay, promotion, and other forms of discrimination and exclusion that testified to the subordinate position envisioned for African Americans in a postemancipation United States. In the process, black soldiers (both those who had been slaves and those who had been free when the Civil War began) and their black and white allies advanced alternative visions of civil and political society that included new ideas of equality, citizenship, and social justice.[23] Indeed, the idea of a slaves' rebellion suggests a potentially different chronology of "Civil War" and "Reconstruction," with a final phase unfolding not before but *after* the official surrender of the Confederacy and the death of Lincoln: as rumors of federal land redistribution swirled through the rural districts—often with the aid of black troops in the army of occupation—and provoked violent encounters between freed people and the reinvigorated white paramilitaries and southern state militias that Lincoln's replacement, Andrew Johnson, had sanctioned. Only with the ratification of the Thirteenth Amendment, the demobilization of black troops, and Congress's assertion of authority over Reconstruction in the winter of 1865–66, which eventuated in legal equality, black male enfranchisement, and a new political order in the former Confederate states, can the slaves' rebellion be said to have ended, and, historically, with stunning success.[24]

However discrete in its unfolding and development, what may be regarded as the slaves' rebellion in the Civil War South did share important features with other—and readily acknowledged—slave rebellions in the Americas. It erupted at a time of bitter division and conflict among the society's white rulers. It depended on networks of communication, intelligence, and interpretation among the slaves. It imagined powerful allies coming to their aid, whose goals and objectives were thought to coincide with theirs. It involved individual and collective acts of flight, not as efforts to redress particular grievances, but as a means of leaving slavery behind and embracing a newly available or imagined freedom. And it ultimately saw slaves take up arms against slaveholders in an attempt to defeat (if not destroy) them and abolish the institution of slavery. In these respects, the slaves' rebellion during the Civil War resonated—showed resemblance at least in part—with the Stono Rebellion of 1739 in South Carolina, with the establishment of maroons in Brazil and Jamaica, with the plot of Gabriel outside Richmond, Virginia, in 1800, with the rising in St. John the Baptist Parish, Louisiana, in 1811, with the Demerara Rebellion of 1823, and with the Jamaican Baptist War of 1831–32, not to mention with what the historian Gary Nash has recently called "the greatest slave rebellion in the history of Great Britain's New World colonies": the flight of thousands of American slaves to British lines during the Revolutionary War.[25]

The slaves of the South did, of course, live and labor in a very distinctive social, political, and cultural environment. Alone among the slaves of the Americas, they were outnumbered by a large, mobile, and armed population of whites who either owned slaves, did the slaveholders' bidding, or wanted little to do with either slaveholders or slaves. Their masters had won independence, created governments and police authorities, and emerged by midcentury as perhaps the most powerful landed elite in the world owing to the market strength of cotton and their own political aggressiveness. And they resided on comparatively small plantations and farms, which made the task of large-scale mobilization exceedingly difficult. The slaves' prospects for achieving anything substantial through organized rebellion at any time between 1815 and 1860 were, in short, about as bleak as could be—as both Nat Turner and John Brown tragically learned—and they seemed to have understood this. Which may be why most of them, having developed understandings and interpretations of the course of national and international events, waited until their imagined allies struck the first blow.

Ironically, the slaves' rebellion during the Civil War

may well be, in its course and outcome, most similar to what we have long considered the greatest and only successful slave rebellion in modern history: the one that exploded in the French colony of Saint Domingue during the 1790s. Although the sugar-growing Caribbean is generally thought to have been a hotbed of slave rebelliousness, Saint Domingue (like the American South) did not have much of a tradition of slave revolt before the late eighteenth century. Aside from endemic marronage and a thwarted slave plot in 1757, the political cauldron was rather on low simmer, and the island became the world's leading producer of sugar and coffee. The precipitant of rebellion, moreover (again as in the United States) was a struggle among whites that initially had nothing to do with the slaves—in this case the French Revolution of 1789. The political opportunity was first seized not by the slaves, but by the free people of color (the *gens de couleur*), who suffered civil and political disabilities despite their service in the colonial militia and the wealth that a good many of them possessed. Their early efforts, clearly influenced by the egalitarian sensibilities of the French revolutionaries, to gain equal standing with whites, not an end to slavery, failed miserably (as did the efforts of free blacks to win civil and political equality in the northern states and to join the Union Army once the war began).[26]

Before long, the slaves on the plantation-dense north coast of Saint Domingue looked to press their own advantage. Their leaders initially sought amelioration rather than emancipation, and they, together with many of their followers, had come to believe that the king of France might be on their side or might have gone so far as to emancipate them, only to be refused on the island by disobedient slaveholders (as many slaves in the American South had come to believe of Lincoln). "The St. Domingue uprising," one historian has remarked, "was one of the first of a new type of slave revolt, soon to be typical, in which the insurgents claimed to be already officially emancipated."[27]

The rebellion itself commenced on the night of August 22, 1791, with a torrent of violence and destruction. Slaves put plantations to the torch, killed or drove off their owners or managers, forced reluctant slaves to join them (and brutally punished those who resisted), and battled the military forces of their masters and of France with a fury that one scholar described as "jihadlike onslaughts."[28] It seemed an almost classic case of what we might expect a slave revolt to be, and surely very different from what transpired in the Civil War South. But Saint Domingue and the American South were very different places, with very different racial demographics, forms of social and economic organization, and political cultures. The slaves in Saint Domingue, most of whom were African born, **outnumbered the free population** (white and mulatto) by more than seven to one. They labored on large sugar plantations owned by absentees and therefore under the direct control of hired managers. And they were first led by slaves deeply influenced by Vodou, if they were not Vodou priests themselves. Had their rebellion gone the way of all others before—crushed militarily within days or weeks—there would be nothing more to compare.

Yet the rebellion in Saint Domingue did not go the way of all others before it. Although by December 1791 one of the slave leaders was dead and the others were suing for peace, the rebellion was reinvigorated by the obstinacy of local authorities and, especially, by events in revolutionary France, which moved in ever more radical directions. Within a year, the French government had extended civil and political equality to the *gens de couleur* and sent a delegation of commissioners to Saint Domingue to enforce its decree; the slave rebels had embraced the goal of freedom for all the enslaved; and a free man of color who had

once been a slave (and had been among the early rebel leaders) named Toussaint Breda (later Louverture) had emerged as a general of what was now a
slave army—an army that had grown in size owing to
widespread *petit marronage,* or flight from the plantations.

The following two years, 1793 and 1794, proved especially decisive. They began with Britain and Spain
declaring war on France, and with the Spanish, from
their base in neighboring Santo Domingo (like the
British during the American Revolution), hoping to
attract the armed slave insurgents to their side by
offering them freedom. The insurgent leaders, including Toussaint, and ten thousand of their troops
quickly took them up on it. French officials in Saint
Domingue were consequently forced to respond, and
they did by initially agreeing to manumit any slave
who would fight for France, and then, in the summer
of 1793, by moving toward a general emancipation
accompanied by the rights of French citizenship.
When, several months later, in the winter of 1794, the
revolutionary government in Paris effectively ratified
what had happened on the ground in Saint Domingue (a roughly similar process to how the Emancipation Proclamation unfolded, though far more generous in political terms), Toussaint left the Spanish

Pitched battle in Saint Domingue between slaves and French soldiers, 1802.

Engraving by Pierre Martinet, Courtesy of Bridgeman-Giraudon/Art Resource, NY.

and some of his rebel allies behind and cast his lot with the French. With him came Henri Christophe (who, like Toussaint, had been free), Moyse, and Jean-Jacques Dessalines (both of whom had been slaves).

Over the next few years, as a military and political leader, Toussaint sent the Spanish and the British down to defeat, became commander-in-chief of the French army in Saint Domingue, and struggled over the direction his rebellion-turned-revolution would take. Pressure came both from the *gens de couleur,* who wanted property rights and commercial dynamism restored, and from the now ex-slaves who wanted land of their own to cultivate. For his part, Toussaint, while resolutely committed to the freedom of Saint Domingue's slaves, also believed that their emancipation could be secured only if the island was able to prosper and defend itself. And, to him, that meant rebuilding the plantations and the staple economy, showing "France and all the Nations" that "Saint Domingue would recover all its riches with the work of free hands." Toussaint, that is, wanted the freed people to return to the sugar and coffee estates and work steadily for wages, and he was prepared to use the military to keep them at it. Indeed, a new constitution he soon wrote for the island, which formalized the abolition of slavery, declared Saint Domingue both free and French, and outlawed racial discrimination, also imposed a draconian labor regime and made him governor for life. It was a harbinger of social and political conflicts that would accompany emancipations elsewhere in the Americas, including the Civil War–era United States.

Before very long, Toussaint faced two major challenges. Freed people disappointed by his policies on land and labor staged a series of rebellions along the north coast that, at great cost to him, Toussaint managed to quell. Even more serious, France's new leader, Napoleon Bonaparte, suspicious of Toussaint's political intentions (would he declare independence?), sent out a very large expedition of French troops with secret orders to arrest and deport all black officers and to reimpose slavery in Saint Domingue, Martinique, and Guadeloupe. Toussaint would be trapped, taken into custody, and shipped off to a frigid prison in France's Jura Mountains, where he died in April 1803. But when his followers learned what the French army had in store for them, they reignited their rebellion and stemmed the tide of counterrevolution. Increasingly decimated by disease, what was left of the defeated French army sailed back to France, and on January 1, 1804, Dessalines, one of the remaining rebel leaders and a close associate of Toussaint's, proclaimed the independence of Haiti (from "Ayiti," the Indian name for the island), the second new nation in the Americas.

What had begun, therefore, as an explosive slave revolt (very much unlike the Civil War South) turned into a protracted and complex political process played out on local and international stages. And however different the two slave societies were, however distinctive the specific courses of events, it is possible to identify a number of broad and meaningful similarities. In both Saint Domingue and the Civil War South, rebellion was provoked by massive struggles between powerful groups within the white population and by the belief among slaves that they had allies among white rulers. In both places free people of color had important roles in setting the direction of political conflict and influencing the goals for a postemancipation world. In both places flight from the plantations—marronage—was integral to the rebellions and crucial to the growth and maintenance of liberating armies. In both places, shifting alliances with and battles against large standing armies proved decisive to the rebellions' outcomes. And in both places, the rebellions became social and political revolutions, eventuating in the abolition of slavery, the crushing military defeat of the slave owners, and the effective birth of new nations.[29]

Indeed, it is arguable that the revolution made by slave rebellion was even more far-reaching in the Civil War South than it was in Saint Domingue. Thousands of slaves took part in the rebellion-turned-revolution in Saint Domingue, many more than would take part in the great rebellions to follow in Barbados, Demerara, and Jamaica. But Saint Domingue in 1791 had a total slave population of just under half a million—about the same number of slaves who rebelled against their masters and found their way to Union lines during the course of the Civil War, and only about 12 percent of the total slave population to be found in the United States at the time. Which is to say that the slave rebellion in the Civil War South was by far the greatest of them all, and it took place and helped transform a slave society that was by far the largest, most economically advanced, and most resilient in the Americas.

⁊◌

Could we then have missed what may have been the greatest slave rebellion in modern history? And, if so, how? The coastal Georgia planters and many of their fellow Confederates were certainly not alone in seeing the specters of slave rebellion and revolution—of "Santo Domingo"—all around them. Especially after they joined forces with the Union Army, some slaves and former slaves displayed the political knowledge they had acquired—and perhaps the Atlantic identities they had begun to fashion—and likened their struggles and objectives to those of Toussaint Louverture and the Haitian revolutionaries. "The result of the insurrection in St. Domingo has long been known among the contrabands of the South," a northern chaplain in Port Royal, South Carolina, could observe during the war, and "the name Toussaint L'Overture has been passed from mouth to mouth, until it has become a secret household word." One company of the famed Fifty-fourth Massachusetts regiment thought to name themselves the "Toussaint Guards," and some black troops sang "The Marseillaise" at public gatherings. A correspondent for the *Weekly Anglo-African* urged blacks to "emulate" their brethren in Haiti, while a sympathetic newspaper in Ohio compared "the stubborn heroism of the Louisiana colored guard at Port Hudson to the desperate valor of the negro soldiers at the siege of Crete-a-Pierrot." Some slave rebels-by-flight apparently spoke of Toussaint and the revolution in Haiti when they made it to Union lines, and in 1863 contrabands in New Bern, North Carolina, seem to have established a colony they chose to call "New Hayti."[30]

A broader association with a developing rebellious and revolutionary tradition—with an ongoing struggle for freedom—was articulated as well. Recruiting black soldiers in 1863, Frederick Douglass thus invoked the memories of "Denmark Vesey of Charleston; . . . Nathaniel Turner of Southampton; . . . [and] Shields Green and Copeland, who followed noble John Brown, and fell as glorious martyrs for the cause of the slave." The *New Orleans Tribune,* published by free people of color, some of whom were the descendants of émigrés from Saint Domingue, compared the Civil War to the French Revolution and, reflecting on a wartime convention in the city, "the first political move ever made by the colored people of the state acting in a body," instructed, "We must come out of the revolution not only as emancipationists but as true republicans." When, on January 1, 1864, more than four thousand freed people in the South Carolina low country celebrated their liberation from bondage, they gathered under a banner "which bore the historic names of 'Washington, Adams, Lincoln, John Brown, Toussaint L'Ouverture, and [Robert Gould] Shaw." "I want you to *understand,*" Martin Delany, who had urged Lincoln to organize "an army of blacks, commanded entirely by black officers," and who had named a son after Toussaint, later told his fellow soldiers of the 104th U.S. Colored Troops, "that we would not have become free had we not armed ourselves and fought out our independence."[31]

Yet, very quickly, the writing and memory making

on the Civil War changed in temper and interpretive connection. The language of revolution—and chiefly in a negative sense—was increasingly reserved for describing not the war but the Reconstruction that followed. The emphasis instead came to be placed on the bravery, valor, and nobility of white soldiers on both sides, on a "brothers' war," in an emerging "reconciliationist" narrative that either erased African Americans from a meaningful role or cast them as loyal adherents of the powers that be, whether slave masters or the federal government. There is, in fact, an important sense in which writers and historians, North and South, black and white, seem to have developed a shared investment—whatever else they may have disagreed on—in rejecting the idea that slaves and freed people acted in a rebellious or revolutionary manner, or provoked a revolutionary transformation, during the Civil War.[32]

Not surprisingly, southern white representations of the war, commencing with the popular literature of the war itself, simultaneously detached secession and the Confederacy from the specific defense of slavery while celebrating the loyalty of the slaves, who, it was said, largely protected their owners and distrusted the Yankee invaders. By the 1880s the "faithful" slave had become an icon of Lost Cause

THE GREATEST SLAVE REBELLION

mythology, inspiring calls for official commemoration, and the outrage and betrayal felt by slaveholders when their slaves fled to Union lines had been effectively forgotten. "When the men of the South were nearly all in the army, the negroes were left in large bodies on the plantations," a former Confederate recalled ten years after the surrender. "They might have been insolent, insubordinate, and idle . . . [or] overturned the social and political fabric at any time, *and they knew* all this too. . . . And yet they remained quiet, faithful, and diligent throughout."[33]

Although northern white writers of the postwar period were more likely to regard the Civil War as the product of a moral and political struggle between slavery and freedom, and were more likely to blame the war on the designs of slaveholders and to "wave the bloody shirt," most also embraced the image of the slave who had spurned rebellion. In the *New Englander and Yale Review,* Joseph E. Roy, who recognized "the negroes . . . for their service as soldiers of the Union," nonetheless insisted that "the first item" in "our indebtedness to the negroes . . . is the fact that [they] did not rise in insurrection. It was in their power to have wrought a carnival of blood . . . and the Union army would probably have been turned upon them to put them down." James Ford Rhodes, a midwestern businessman whose work is widely regarded as laying the foundation for the "irrepressible conflict" school of Civil War historiography and who viewed slavery as the war's principal cause, put the slaves' behavior in a similar light. "One of the strange things in this eventful history," he wrote in 1917, "is the peaceful labor of three and one-half million negro slaves whose presence in the South was the cause of the war and whose freedom was fought for after September, 1862, by the Northern soldiers." Quoting Henry Grady's remark that "a thousand torches would have disbanded the Southern army but there was not one," Rhodes added, "Instead of rising [the slaves] remained patiently submissive and faithful to their owners."[34]

The advent of professionalized history writing, in the late nineteenth century, lent further credibility to this perspective. Embracing the spirit of sectional reconciliation as well as the racialist thinking that transcended regional boundaries, academically trained historians offered more dispassionate assessments of the Civil War's causes and course, and they either relegated slaves (and often slavery) to the margins or summoned them only to reinscribe the image of their quiescence. Historians from the South, many trained by Ulrich B. Phillips, were more likely to take up the matter than their northern counterparts, and although some acknowledged that slaves occasionally fled to Union lines or that rumors of insurrection surfaced from time to time, they seemed far more impressed by the slaves' "docility" and "heroic loyalty to their masters." Whether the cause was "love and fidelity," "training and discipline," or limited "capacity for organization," the slaves' failure to rise seemed to confirm a paternalistic interpretation of their enslavement. "Taken as a whole," E. Merton Coulter concluded in his volume *The Confederate States of America,* published in Louisiana State University Press's prestigious History of the South series, "The slaves came through the period of the war with a greater feeling of happiness and well-being than the white people."[35] *Seen as moral good*

African Americans had a very different view of the experience of slavery and the meanings of the Civil War. In their processions, celebrations, political conventions, and eventual formal history writing, they described slavery and emancipation as central to the war, as the great turning point in their own history and a great chapter in the larger history of freedom, as a reflection of divine providence, and as a rebirth of the country's revolutionary principles. And they took special care and pride to highlight the role played by slaves and freed people in the outcome. They spoke of bravery and heroism, danger and sacrifice, patriotism and manhood.[36]

But, with rare exception, they did not speak or write of rebellion and revolution. From the hustings, the pulpits, the newspapers, and the history books, black leaders took pains to stress the order, discipline, responsibility, restraint, and sobriety that were to be found in their wartime communities, and especially among their men. Slaves did not so much rebel against their condition and their masters as come to save the Union in its darkest hour. They were the loyal ones, in thrall to white rebels. They defended the flag while their owners desecrated it. They fought for the nation as they had many times before. Indeed, they *did not rise in rebellion* when the conditions were most auspicious. They did not slaughter their oppressors or burn the plantations and farms. They were civil, their masters barbarous.

There was, and would remain, an important political logic to the narratives of wartime activity that African Americans constructed. They lived in a world in which they had been enslaved, rendered dependent, and excluded from civil and political society; in which they were outnumbered by white people; in which citizenship, opportunity, and power were associated with independence and manliness; and in which black men with guns, acting on their own, struck the most desperate fears in the hearts of the white majority. Emancipation coming in the midst of civil war not only gave African Americans the chance to represent themselves as liberators of their own people. It also provided an unprecedented opening for them to bid for rights that had been denied, for an inclusion that had been impossible to achieve, for safety and security so necessary to their development as individuals, families, and communities.

It therefore made sense for orators, editors, and historians (a few sympathetic whites as well as blacks) to craft stories of black agency that simultaneously dispelled racist caricatures and encouraged admiration, all the more so as the rights and power that African Americans gained during Reconstruction came under increasingly ferocious attack. Some bent over backward to find a conciliatory posture, speaking, as Booker T. Washington did, of the "thousands of . . . homeless and helpless people [who] fell into the hands of the Federal commanders" during the Civil War. The historian Charles Wesley went so far as to align the sentiments of the slaves with "the South" at large. "To the majority of the Negroes," he wrote in the *Journal of Negro History* in 1919, "the invading ar-

mies of the Union seemed to be ruthlessly attack-
ing independent States, invading the homeland and
tramping upon all that those men held dear . . . [so
that] the Negroes were not only loyal in remaining at
home and doing their duty but also in offering themselves for actual service in the Confederate army."
But most others combined recognition of black service to the Union and their people with emphasis on
black civility, self-respect, courtesy, and cooperation.
"That the slaves did not rise in their tens of thousands to slaughter their masters in their homes during the war," one powerfully proclaimed, "is not evidence of loyalty but rather of civilized self-restraint."
In so doing, they anticipated the revisionist writings
on slavery, abolitionism, and Reconstruction that
would not surface in any numbers for another two or
three decades.[37]

The great exception to these interpretive sensibilities was W. E. B. Du Bois's *Black Reconstruction in
America, 1860–1880,* published in 1935. It was not simply, as the book's lengthy subtitle announced, that
his was "an essay toward a history of the part which
black folk played in the attempt to reconstruct democracy in America." It was also that he regarded
African Americans, under slavery and freedom, as
consequential political actors. Thus, during the Civil

War, the slaves, in Du Bois's telling, did not just re-
act or respond to new circumstances. Rather, they
"crouched consciously and moved silently, listening,
hoping and hesitating." "It must be borne in mind
that nine-tenths of the four million black slaves
could neither read nor write, and that the overwhelming majority of them were isolated on country
plantations," he cautioned. "Any mass movement under such circumstances must materialize slowly and
painfully. . . . The Negroes showed no disposition to
strike the one terrible blow which brought black men
freedom in Haiti and which in all history has been
used by slaves and justified." Yet, when the slaves finally determined to their satisfaction that "the Union
armies would not or could not return fugitive slaves,
and that their masters with all their fume and fury
were uncertain of victory," they acted collectively,
in immense numbers, taking flight from their plantations and offering their "services to the Federal
Army," in effect withdrawing their labor from their
masters and the Confederacy and bestowing it on the
Union. This act of political self-consciousness, which
"decided the war," Du Bois (reflecting the Marxism
he at the time embraced) termed a "general strike."[38]

Although it would be another three decades (or
more) before *Black Reconstruction*'s influence would

become apparent, a new era of African American historiography was about to take shape. Volumes in the 1940s and 1950s by John Hope Franklin, Benjamin Quarles, and Dudley Taylor Cornish—building on the earlier accounts of George Washington Williams and Joseph T. Wilson—spotlighted the contributions of slaves and freed people, especially in the Union armed forces, to the advent of emancipation and the defeat of the Confederacy.[39] Revisionist writing on the coming of the Civil War and on Reconstruction in the 1950s and 1960s tended to focus on white abolitionists and Radical Republicans, giving them the sympathetic hearing that scholars had generally denied them since the late nineteenth century.[40] But it was a dramatically new engagement with slavery that made it possible for historians to move in the direction that Du Bois had marked out. Beginning with Kenneth Stampp's *Peculiar Institution,* and then taking off in the 1970s with a series of remarkable studies of slaves and their transition to freedom—by John Blassingame, Eugene Genovese, Herbert Gutman, Lawrence Levine, Nathan Huggins, and Leon Litwack—historians showed growing and increasingly sophisticated interest in what slaves "did" under slavery, and in how they shaped the institution and hastened its eventual demise.[41] By the 1980s, as emphasis shifted to the Civil War and Reconstruction, the shadow of Du Bois was unmistakably in evidence. Indeed, it was hard to find a historian who did not pay Du Bois deep homage.[42]

Nonetheless, while embracing the figure of Du Bois, historians—Marxists among them—largely rejected one of the conceptual centerpieces of *Black Reconstruction:* the idea of the "general strike." Some explicitly dismissed the idea, either on theoretical, empirical, or outright political grounds. Most just ignored it. Few, if any, took the occasion to engage with it in any sustained or meaningful way. Does the idea of a general strike of the slaves during the Civil War make any sense? If not, what are the problems with it, and can we find anything in the formulation that would better help us understand what the slaves undertook? To be sure, scholars are no longer reluctant to describe the many ways in which slaves pursued their freedom during the Civil War, and they often use language and rubrics evocative of rebellion. They write of "moments of truth," of "black liberators," and of "self-emancipation." They have even engaged in a sharp debate over whether the slaves "freed themselves."[43] But the idea of "rebellion" has been sidestepped or disowned. In a pioneering study on "the aftermath of slavery," whose rich documentation frequently suggests otherwise, the historian Leon Litwack thus writes: "The fact remains that the slaves failed to execute a major rebellion," that there was an "absence of any major slave revolts during the Civil War."[44]

෨෮

When freed people assembled in local meetings and statewide conventions during the summer and fall of 1865 to press their claims for freedom and equal rights and to fend off charges that they intended to rise up and seize lands they believed the government had promised them, they sketched a collective self-portrait designed to offer them citizenship in the republic and protection from violence. They spoke movingly of the oppression they had suffered under slavery and, especially, of the loyalty they had shown the Union during the Civil War. "In the darkest hour of American history when treason and rebellion swept over the South," they had "remained loyal to the Government of the United States" and "gladly came forth to fight her battles, and to protect the flag that had enslaved" them. They had "flocked to [federal] lines," provided "valuable information," guided "your scouting parties and minor expeditions," dug "your trenches," drove "your teams," and, when permitted, showed "heroism . . . at Ft. Wagner, Port Hudson, Milliken's Bend, and before Petersburg and Richmond." Through it all, they had been "law-abiding subjects," seeking "to conduct" themselves so that "no just cause of complaint may exist," rejecting "insurrection" after the war as they had during it. "Rebellion" described their masters' actions, not their own.[45]

These arguments were both powerfully felt and politically astute. They revealed a familiarity with the political culture of the nineteenth-century United States and with the associations that composed the bases of belonging and citizenship: loyalty, independence, discipline, manhood, military service. And in various forms the arguments would continue to be deployed as African Americans struggled for their rights and against the many constraints and disabilities of racism. Indeed, they have been so powerful and compelling, so politically and morally righteous, that sympathetic historians have, for the most part, fully embraced them in constructing narratives of the nation's past, which may be one reason they have been so reluctant to find "rebellion" in what black people did during the Civil War. They seem to be more comfortable writing of the slaves' *escape from* their oppression and *pursuit of* freedom through established institutional channels, even if slaves and freed people thereby brought to light the racism and discrimination that those institutions sanctioned. At the very least, the emphasis would then be on African Americans' desire for integration, their identification with the country's professed ideals, and their acceptance of officially recognized political practices; it would not be on their potential resort to "insurrection" or their interest in different goals and values, which would be politically far more complex, if not far more dangerous.

Yet there may be an even deeper, more philosophical and conceptual explanation for historians' dismissing or ignoring the possibility of a Civil War slave rebellion. And that is their general refusal to regard slaves as genuine political people. Historians would, of course, easily admit that slaves are fully able to register their desires and discontents, to baffle, exasperate, or please their owners, and to behave in ways that force those who are regarded as political people in their society to act publicly: to write laws, raise panics, make policies, start wars, and conquer new territories. But what the slaves themselves do— their part in the South's or the nation's political dramas—is, rather, labeled "resistance" or "accommodation," and thus as "pre-political." "Politics" comes to them only as slavery is in the process of ending, and it is brought in by those who were never, or who were no longer, slaves. *mutually exclusive*

There seems to be something quintessentially American about this intellectual disposition, for those who study slave societies in the Caribbean and Brazil, or those who study peasant societies in Europe, Latin America, Africa, and south Asia, tend to take a far more expansive view of the potential cast of political actors. Hilary McD. Beckles, a historian of slavery in the British West Indies, can therefore write of the links that existed "between plantation-based politics and the international anti-slavery ethos," and suggest that the many slave struggles that erupted between 1638 and 1838 can "be conceived of as the '200 Years' War,'" a protracted battle "launched by Africans and their Afro–West Indian progeny against slave owners."[46] In the United States, perhaps, the early importance of electoral methods, the respect for legal and constitutional determinations, and the formal exclusion of slaves from civil and political society have together impelled historians to adopt the perspectives of those who could hold the franchise at the time: that slaves were simply outside anything we would recognize as politics.

The price we pay for this, and the prospects we de-fer, may be considerable. Raising the possibility of slave rebellion during the Civil War may very well not end with a new and persuasive argument. Most historians may remain convinced that "rebellion" or "revolt" or "insurrection" does not reasonably characterize what the slaves did and did not do. But such an inquiry would require us to imagine a much larger universe of politics, to look seriously at the political participation and influence of those who are formally excluded from the arena of electoral activity, and to explore the connections between the electoral and other arenas of political life. In the process, we may discover ways to incorporate the ideas that have come out of women's and gender history, Native American history, and transnational or comparative history into a dramatically different political panorama. We may, that is, develop the questions, skills, insights, and methods to begin writing a political history that would truly be "new."

3

MARCUS GARVEY, THE UNIA, AND THE HIDDEN POLITICAL HISTORY OF AFRICAN AMERICANS

Late in the winter of 2005, I saw a notice in a Philadelphia paper for an upcoming exhibit on Marcus Garvey and his organization, the Universal Negro Improvement Association (or the UNIA). The exhibit was to be on display at the African-American Museum in Center City, and it was scheduled for several hours on a Saturday afternoon. At the time, I thought it odd that a museum exhibit would be up for a mere afternoon, but I was very much interested in Garvey and his movement and eager to see what might be there, so I decided to go.

When I entered the museum that Saturday and explained that I wished to see the Garvey exhibit, I was directed to a lower floor. There I entered a space that was packed, not with photographs, documents, or other memorabilia, but with people—a great many of them, all seemingly of African descent, from the very young to the quite elderly. They were seated in folding chairs (or standing around them) on the floor before a small stage where, at the moment I entered, some of the children, of elementary school age, were performing a skit about Marcus Garvey, much to the delight of the very attentive audience. When the children finished, a tall, very striking-looking black man in a dark suit rose to speak, and as he did I learned that I had not walked into a museum exhibit on Garvey and the UNIA at all; I had instead walked into a meeting of the Philadelphia branch of the UNIA.

I had no idea that the UNIA, which Garvey founded in Jamaica in 1914 and which had its heyday in the United States in the late 1910s and 1920s, was still in existence and, obviously, drawing crowds of followers. And virtually everyone I subsequently told about this event, including scholars who work in the field of African American history, expressed similar astonishment. This was clearly news to them. But it probably shouldn't have been. Along with the one in Philadelphia, there are currently UNIA divisions in Washington, D.C., Richmond, metropolitan Atlanta (three of them), metropolitan Chicago (also three), Cleveland, Los Angeles, Detroit, Durham, and Baltimore, as well as Montreal, Dakar, Port Harcourt

(Nigeria), Bergvlei (South Africa), Montego Bay, and Kingston; and although some of the divisions may have been reorganized relatively recently, there is every reason to think that most hark back to the UNIA's founding.[1]

Thus, there is a deep history of the UNIA about which we know very little, though this seems emblematic of a larger and more curious elision: that is to say, how little we know, at any point in its history, about what is acknowledged to be the greatest mass movement of people of African descent in the twentieth century. Garvey himself has, of course, drawn a good deal of attention, and thanks to the labors of Robert A. Hill and his associates we now have ten of the projected twelve volumes of the papers of Marcus Garvey and the UNIA.[2] Yet there has been only one new biography of Garvey in the past half century; there have been no major histories of the movement, very few oral histories of people who regarded themselves as Garveyites, and almost nothing about the local experience of Garveyism and the UNIA outside New York, where Garvey had his headquarters before he was imprisoned for mail fraud and then deported.[3] Representations of the social basis of the UNIA are largely conjectural (and often contradictory), and only a handful of scholars have bothered to study either the geographic expanse of the organization or the character and activities of the membership in any one place.[4] To the question why so many thousands of African Americans (not to mention African Caribbeans and Africans) were drawn to Garvey's message and his movement—and would continue to be drawn to it well after Garvey's own demise—and to the question what people heard and how what they heard resonated with and transformed their sensibilities, the answers are few and, for the most part, unsatisfying.[5]

The limitations in our knowledge and understanding of Garveyism and the UNIA would be comprehensible if the movement were fleeting and relatively superficial. But this was hardly the case. Garveyism won massive support in the 1920s, and its intellectual and political legacies have been profound. It left its mark on every major black social and political movement of the twentieth century (here and abroad) and was an influence (often the dominant influence) on every form of popular black nationalism in the United States from the Nation of Islam to the Black Panthers. Elijah Muhammad came into early contact with Garveyites, and Malcolm X grew up in a household of them. John Hope Franklin remembers how avidly Garvey's newspaper, the *Negro World,* was read in the black section of Tulsa when he was a boy. Members of the Industrial and Commercial Workers Union in the South African Transkei imagined, in the late 1920s, that Garveyites would be arriving from America by ship and air to support their struggles, and Garvey's call for "Africa for the Africans" helped energize anticolonial mobilizations throughout the continent. Some leaders of the Black Panther Party carried Garvey's writings and instructed recruits to study them. And there can be little doubt that Garveyism established a popular base among black Americans to rival that of the NAACP, or that Garvey-inflected black nationalist ideas continue to have great currency among black workers and the black poor.[6]

Yet, for all this, studies of W. E. B. Du Bois and the NAACP, of black union organizing and black communists, of black middle-class politics and institutions, and of the Civil Rights movement in its national, regional, and local incarnations abound, while Garvey and the UNIA are often summoned only to be marginalized, dismissed, or derided. An immense world of politics, ideas, and cultural practices, which may complicate or confound our views of the past century, thereby remains largely hidden from us. And although the challenges of research have helped keep much of this world from view, the main culprits are scholars and intellectuals who have chosen not to see.

ॐ

It isn't easy to get beyond square one. Considerations of Garveyism and the UNIA naturally begin with Garvey himself, a figure who has, for the most part, been vilified, disparaged, scorned, and lampooned. Observers at the time (including a fair share of African American intellectuals and political leaders, beginning with Du Bois) and many scholars since have depicted Garvey in derisive and almost comical terms: as a foreigner out of touch with American life; as a political dreamer who misled his followers; as a scam artist looking to fleece the masses and line his pockets; as something of a religious revivalist who traded on the traditions of faith and fraternalism; as a racial purist whose dangerous sensibilities led him to political associations with white supremacists; and as a self-absorbed and self-referential buffoon, outfitting himself and his African Legion with silly, resplendent military attire in pathetic mimicry of the colonial powers that were. That he attracted so much attention makes Garvey all the more problematic and his movement something of an embarrassment. How could the UNIA be anything but a collection of angry, ignorant, unsophisticated, and displaced black folk, easily duped by the veneer of authority and the offer of community? Small wonder that Garvey's principal adherents are often made out to be West Indians, recently arrived from the islands.[7]

Finding one's way through this thicket of representation to a clearer sense of Garveyism and the UNIA is a formidable task, which may help explain why there have been few takers. Unlike the records of the NAACP and its operations locally and nationally, which are voluminous, well-organized, and very substantial, those of Garvey and the UNIA are far thinner. The published papers focus on Garvey, his writings, speeches, and doings, the many ways in which he was harassed by federal and local authorities for what they regarded as his threatening activities, his conflicts with African American leaders, and his growing legal problems. There is also a good deal on the UNIA's structure, its annual conventions, and its divisions in large cities such as New York, Philadelphia, Chicago, and Los Angeles. The unpublished records, housed in the Schomburg Center for Research in Black Culture in New York City, are relatively scanty (six microfilm rolls' worth) and chiefly spotlight the activities and correspondence of the Central Division in New York. The UNIA did publish a weekly newspaper, the *Negro World,* which printed reports from divisions all over the United States and the world and had a Spanish-language page, but it has long been regarded as little more than Garvey's mouthpiece and propaganda organ.

Still, there is much with which to work. Garvey's speeches, editorials, and correspondence, which may be found both in his published papers and in the *Negro World,* reward close readings because they show a political vision in an almost continuous state of evolution and because his ideas and plans bear little resemblance to the ways they have been represented and caricatured. The unpublished papers, moreover, include several boxes of index cards, which provide information on the UNIA's many divisions in the United States, the Caribbean, Central America, and Africa in the mid- to late 1920s: the location, the division number (which gives a sense of when it was organized), the names of the president and secretary, and occasionally the membership. Further information on members and sympathizers can be obtained in the pages of the *Negro World,* which not only published letters to the editor but routinely listed the names and hometowns of men and women (many hundreds of them) who contributed even a few cents to Garvey's various causes—especially to his legal defense fund. All this material combines to yield a far richer portrait of Garvey, Garveyism, and the UNIA than we currently have, and, even more, one that is challenging and surprising in its meanings and implications.

Perhaps the greatest surprises concern the movement's geographic and social base. The UNIA has long been seen as an organization of the urban North, a testimony to the effect of the Great Migration as well as to the arrival of thousands of West Indian immigrants in the first two decades of the twentieth century. And there is no question that, in terms of total members, the UNIA divisions in New York, Philadelphia, and Chicago were among the largest; New York easily had pride of place (as many as thirty thousand members). But the picture is very different if we consider the number of divisions and where most of them were to be found.[8]

The growth of the UNIA was nothing short of explosive. Garvey arrived in the United States in the spring of 1916 intending to raise money for a Jamaican school modeled after Booker T. Washington's Tuskegee Normal and Industrial Institute in Alabama. Indeed, Garvey had corresponded with Washington and initially planned his American trip around meeting with him, but Washington died unexpectedly in 1915. Garvey decided to come to the United States anyway, hoping, in part, to see Washington's successors and secure financial support from them; but shortly after landing in New York, he set off on a thirty-eight-state tour of visiting and lecturing. By the time he returned to New York, he was more interested in advancing the prospects of the UNIA, which had never taken off in Jamaica. He quickly established a division in Harlem and began publishing the *Negro World*, which was soon circulating in black communities not only across much of the United States, but also throughout much of the Atlantic world.[9]

By 1922 the UNIA could boast more than a thousand divisions, and there would be further growth through the 1920s, even after Garvey's incarceration. Well over two hundred of the divisions were outside the United States: in southern and western Africa, including South Africa, Gold Coast, Nigeria, Liberia, and Sierra Leone; in South America, including Brazil, Venezuela, and Ecuador; across Canada, from Nova Scotia and Quebec to British Columbia; and particularly in the Caribbean basin, where much activity was in evidence, especially in Panama, Costa Rica, British Honduras, Trinidad, Jamaica, Guatemala, and Cuba. The reach of the *Negro World*—thanks in good part to black maritime laborers, sailors, and soldiers—came to be so great in the years after World War I, and to appear so threatening to the stability of colonial regimes, that officials from Cape Town to Lagos to Belize and to Port-of-Spain moved to ban its distribution. It made some sense for them to do that. The *Negro World* was a spark (usually the main spark) in organizing UNIA divisions, and the paper was customarily read to those who attended the division meetings.[10]

Yet about three-quarters of the UNIA divisions (over 900) operated within the borders of the United States, and most of them were neither in the Northeast, the Middle Atlantic, nor the Midwest, nor were they in large urban areas. Rather, the majority of the UNIA divisions were in the former slave states of the South, and the great majority of them were to be found in small towns, villages, and rural areas. (See table 1 in the appendix.) Louisiana had more divisions than any other state in the nation (75), and it was followed by the southern state of North Carolina (61) and the middle Atlantic state of Pennsylvania (61). The only other northern states in the top ten were New Jersey (41) and Ohio (40). California (22) and New York (19) ranked sixteenth and seventeenth, respectively, behind Oklahoma (31), Missouri (30),

Florida (30), Illinois (26), and South Carolina (25), and well behind Mississippi (56), Arkansas (42), and Georgia (35).[11]

New Orleans proved to be a hotbed of UNIA organizing, and many divisions grew up in and around the city, or in the towns and country districts of the surrounding sugar bowl. The same was true of Norfolk and Newport News, Virginia, Charleston, South Carolina, and Miami, Florida, where hundreds of dues payers could be attracted and Sunday evening meetings would pack respective "Liberty Halls."[12] But elsewhere in Virginia, and in North Carolina, Alabama, Georgia, Mississippi, Arkansas, and Missouri, the divisions were overwhelmingly rural, located in the Tidewater, in the old tobacco and cotton belts, and in the new cotton frontier of the Mississippi Delta.[13] Their memberships were generally of small or modest size. The UNIA required at least seven "members of the Negro race [displaying] . . . sufficient intelligence as to safeguard the interests of the society" before it would grant a charter, and though the dues were not to exceed twenty-five cents per month, that was clearly beyond the resources of most rural and small-town African Americans.[14]

Many of the southern divisions, therefore, had somewhere between ten and thirty members at any one time, although this offers only a baseline estimate of Garvey's support. Local UNIA meetings and conventions could bring impressive turnouts—such as the 1,500 who showed up in Merigold, Mississippi (population 606), or the 10,000 who reportedly gathered in Pelham, Georgia (population 2,640)—and the *Negro World* circulated much more widely than the UNIA divisions and got into many more hands than those of direct subscribers. "I am not a member of the UNIA but a well wisher," began a typical letter to the editor, this from Ross, Texas. A meeting in Baxley, Georgia (population 1,142), in August 1923, called to protest the legal "injustice" being done to Marcus Garvey, brought only a small crowd owing to threats of local harassment but also 200 signatures on a petition. Indeed, of nearly 3,400 individuals who contributed small amounts of money to the UNIA during the year 1923, almost 1,900, or 55 percent, lived in the southern states. (See table 1 in the appendix.)[15]

The social composition of UNIA divisions—as best as can be determined at this point—varied, in part, according to the demographic character of the places in which they were located. West Indians figured prominently in New York, Boston, and south Florida (mostly Bahamians in Miami and its vicinity), and to a much lesser extent in Philadelphia and Pittsburgh.

Southern migrants were centrally important in Hartford, Jersey City, Chicago, Cleveland, Dayton, Detroit,
and Los Angeles: in fact, in virtually every city and
town outside the South, where, together, they composed nearly three-quarters of Garvey's supporters.
(See table 2 in the appendix.) And in the urban areas
generally, the UNIA appears to have attracted a range
of petit bourgeois and working-class African Americans.

But almost everywhere, the rank and file of the
UNIA seemed to be composed disproportionately of
black workers and their families who sought or had
attained some measure of respectability. In cities and
towns—North, South, and West—they tended to be
factory and railroad workers, longshoremen, ship-
yard workers, porters, waiters, tradesmen, domestics,
and wage laborers. In the countryside, they might be
lumber or turpentine workers, coal miners, or railroad section hands, though they were more likely to
be tenants and farm laborers (with a scattering of
farm owners, especially in the Upper South) in districts that raised cotton, sugar, and tobacco. (See table 3 in the appendix.) The men and women tended
to be older (at least in their thirties and forties), to
be married or widowed, to be literate, and to have
sent their children to school. In the South they over-

whelmingly resided in the states in which they (and often their parents) had been born, and they seem to have lived in a locale for a good stretch of time and to have achieved some economic stability, even if it involved mortgages or debt that also tied them to the land. (See tables 2 and 4 in the appendix.) In Marcus Garvey and the UNIA, they—South, North, and West—appear to have heard voices, ideas, and plans that resonated with their experiences and aspirations.[16]

ळ्ळ

During the years of the UNIA's most rapid growth—1918-1922—Marcus Garvey presented an argument and a set of projects that simultaneously took sobering account of African American prospects in the depths of the Jim Crow era and offered a breathtaking vision of political struggle and redemption. He seemed to be especially inspired by the World War I moment, not only because it brought a ferocious racist outburst in the United States but also because of the political transformations it appeared to be unleashing internationally. Irish nationalism, Zionism, the Russian Revolution, the Versailles Peace Conference, and Pan-Africanism heralded both a dramatic shake-up of the old order and the possibility of creating something new. People of African descent, Garvey believed, had to ready themselves, to "make up our minds now," to play a central role in history's unfolding.[17]

First and foremost, that would mean retaking their homeland of Africa. The world, as Garvey had come to see it, was organized around races, nations, and empires. African peoples—whether on the continent or elsewhere in the diaspora—had fallen subject to the rule and exploitation of whites, and "no race can be completely free, living as subjects of an alien race." It would be a "big mistake," he insisted, to "think that the white man is going to be more liberal" or that blacks could successfully achieve equality in societies dominated by whites. They would continue to be lynched and mobbed and ground down until their oppressors had to answer to power—to a black nation with the muscle to defend itself and command the world's respect. "Some serious attempt must be made," Garvey told a UNIA meeting in New York, "to build up a government and a nation sufficiently strong to protect the Negro or your future in the U.S. will not be worth a snap of a finger. . . . [W]ithout an independent Africa, without a powerful Africa you are lost."[18]

Like the Irish struggle of the time, to which he

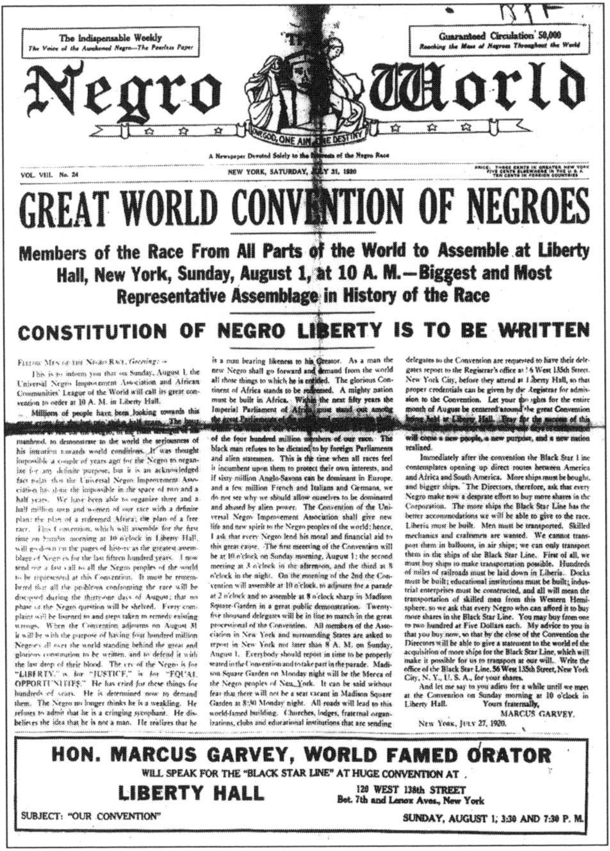

The Indispensable Weekly
The Voice of the Awakened Negro—The Peerless Paper

Guaranteed Circulation 50,000
Reaching the Mass of Negroes Throughout the World

Negro World

ONE GOD, ONE AIM, ONE DESTINY

A Newspaper Devoted Solely to the Interests of the Negro Race

VOL. VIII. No. 24 NEW YORK, SATURDAY, JULY 31, 1920

PRICE: THREE CENTS IN GREATER NEW YORK; FIVE CENTS ELSEWHERE IN THE U. S. A.; TEN CENTS IN FOREIGN COUNTRIES

GREAT WORLD CONVENTION OF NEGROES

Members of the Race From All Parts of the World to Assemble at Liberty Hall, New York, Sunday, August 1, at 10 A. M.—Biggest and Most Representative Assemblage in History of the Race

CONSTITUTION OF NEGRO LIBERTY IS TO BE WRITTEN

FELLOW MEN OF THE NEGRO RACE, *Greeting:—*

This is to inform you that on Sunday, August 1, the Universal Negro Improvement Association and African Communities' League of the World will call its great convention to order at 10 A. M. in Liberty Hall.

Millions of people have been looking towards this [illegible] manhood, to demonstrate to the world the seriousness of his intention towards world conditions. It was thought impossible a couple of years ago for the Negro to organize for any definite purpose, but it is an acknowledged fact today that the Universal Negro Improvement Association has done the impossible in the space of two and a half years. We have been able to organize three and a half million men and women of our race with a definite plan: the plan of a redeemed Africa; the plan of a free race. This Convention, which will assemble for the first time on Sunday morning at 10 o'clock in Liberty Hall, will go down on the pages of history as the greatest assemblage of Negroes for the last fifteen hundred years. I now send out a last call to all the Negro peoples of the world to be represented at this Convention. It must be remembered that all the problems confronting the race will be discussed during the thirty-one days of August; that no phase of the Negro question will be shelved. Every complaint will be listened to and steps taken to remedy existing wrongs. When the Convention adjourns on August 31 it will be with the purpose of having four hundred million Negroes all over the world standing behind the great and glorious constitution to be written, and to defend it with the last drop of their blood. The cry of the Negro is for "LIBERTY," is for "JUSTICE," is for "EQUAL OPPORTUNITIES." He has cried for these things for hundreds of years. He is determined now to demand them. The Negro no longer thinks he is a weakling. He refuses to admit that he is a cringing sycophant. He disbelieves the idea that he is not a man. He realizes that he is a man bearing likeness to his Creator. As a man the new Negro shall go forward and demand from the world all those things to which he is entitled. The glorious Continent of Africa stands to be redeemed. A mighty nation must be built in Africa. Within the next fifty years the Imperial Parliament of Africa must stand out among [illegible] of the four hundred million members of our race. The black man refuses to be dictated to by foreign Parliaments and alien statesmen. This is the time when all races feel it incumbent upon them to protect their own interests, and if sixty million Anglo-Saxons can be dominant in Europe, and a few million French and Italians and Germans, we do not see why we should allow ourselves to be dominated and abused by alien power. The Convention of the Universal Negro Improvement Association shall give new life and new spirit to the Negro peoples of the world; hence, I ask that every Negro lend his moral and financial aid to this great cause. The first meeting of the Convention will be at 10 o'clock on Sunday morning, August 1; the second meeting at 3 o'clock in the afternoon, and the third at 8 o'clock in the night. On the morning of the 2nd the Convention will assemble at 10 o'clock, to adjourn for a parade at 2 o'clock and to assemble at 8 o'clock sharp in Madison Square Garden in a great public demonstration. Twenty-five thousand delegates will be in line to march in the great processional of the Convention. All members of the Association in New York and surrounding States are asked to report in New York not later than 8 A. M. on Sunday, August 1. Everybody should report in time to be properly seated in the Convention and to take part in the parade. Madison Square Garden on Monday night will be the Mecca of the Negro peoples of New York. It can be said without fear that there will not be a seat vacant in Madison Square Garden at 8:30 Monday night. All roads will lead to this world-famed building. Churches, lodges, fraternal organizations, clubs and educational institutions that are sending delegates to the Convention are requested to have their delegates report to the Registrar's office at 56 West 135th Street, New York City, before they attend at Liberty Hall, so that proper credentials can be given by the Registrar for admission to the Convention. Let your thoughts for the entire month of August be centered around the great Convention being held at Liberty Hall. Pray for the success of this [illegible] will come a new people, a new purpose, and a new nation realized.

Immediately after the convention the Black Star Line contemplates opening up direct routes between America and Africa and South America. More ships must be bought, and bigger ships. The Directors, therefore, ask that every Negro make now a desprate effort to buy more shares in the Corporation. The more ships the Black Star Line has the better accommodations we will be able to give to the race. Liberia must be built. Men must be transported. Skilled mechanics and craftsmen are wanted. We cannot transport them in balloons, in air ships; we can only transport them in the ships of the Black Star Line. First of all, we must buy ships to make transportation possible. Hundreds of miles of railroads must be laid down in Liberia. Docks must be built; educational institutions must be built; industrial enterprises must be constructed, and all will mean the transportation of skilled men from this Western Hemisphere, so we ask that every Negro who can afford it to buy more shares in the Black Star Line. You may buy from one to two hundred at Five Dollars each. My advice to you is that you buy now, so that by the close of the Convention the Directors will be able to give a statement to the world of the acquisition of more ships for the Black Star Line, which will make it possible for us to transport at our will. Write the office of the Black Star Line, 56 West 135th Street, New York City, N. Y., U. S. A., for your shares.

And let me say to you adieu for a while until we meet at the Convention on Sunday morning at 10 o'clock in Liberty Hall.

Yours fraternally,
MARCUS GARVEY.

NEW YORK, JULY 27, 1920.

HON. MARCUS GARVEY, WORLD FAMED ORATOR
WILL SPEAK FOR THE "BLACK STAR LINE" AT HUGE CONVENTION AT
LIBERTY HALL 120 WEST 138th STREET
Bet. 7th and Lenox Aves., New York
SUBJECT: "OUR CONVENTION" SUNDAY, AUGUST 1; 3:30 AND 7:30 P. M.

The *Negro World,* newspaper of the UNIA.

Courtesy of the Marcus Garvey and Universal Negro Improvement Association Papers Project, UCLA.

was drawn, Garvey's vision was nationalist and anti-colonial. He called not so much for African repatriation as for a movement to oust the European colonizers and to establish a basis for black self-governance, a movement that would link "every member of the race in every part of the world" who, wherever their residence, were "citizens" of Africa. "We of the UNIA," he proclaimed, "are not endeavoring to repatriate at the present moment . . . twelve million Negroes of America, or twelve or fifteen million from the West Indies, . . . [or] twenty-five millions in South and Central America. . . . We are first trying to organize these [millions] . . . with the one object of a free and redeemed Africa." Garvey acknowledged that such an undertaking would require time, that "we have years before us," perhaps "a hundred years," until "Africa finds a Napoleon" and "we will march from this Western Hemisphere sixty million strong." Nonetheless, he was "preaching preparedness." As a Garveyite in Los Angeles later recalled, "Mr. Garvey never did advocate for all Negroes to go back to Africa. [No] he never did that. He was teaching the people that as long as you're in somebody else's house you can't rule . . . [and] Africa was the only continent in which they could have a government of their own."[19]

Yet the UNIA was to be more than the vehicle of

organization and preparedness; it was also imagined as an embryonic form of the new African nation itself, a government in exile. "We are endeavoring to perform the function of the government of our race," Garvey announced, "just as the Government of America performs the function of government for ninety million white people." To that end, the UNIA drew up a constitution and a "declaration of rights," created an African Legion and a Black Cross Nursing Corps, recognized organizational units by the military term "divisions," invested in factories, laundries, and restaurants, discussed the wisdom of a "civil service" to avoid corruption and train a political class, established the Black Star Shipping Line to move people and goods in what was seen as a global political economy, looked to ally itself with the government of Liberia, paraded in large processions, sang an anthem and waved a national flag (red, black, and green), and made Marcus Garvey provisional president. "If we are to rise as a great people to become a great national force," Garvey declared, "we must start business enterprises of our own; we must build ships and start trading with ourselves between America, the West Indies, and Africa. We must put up factories in all the great manufacturing centers of the country . . . and in these factories we must manufacture . . . all the necessities of life, those things that people need, not only our people . . . but the people of China, of India, of South and Central America, and even the white man." Eventually, "we must have an African Army second to none and a Navy second to none," so that "if they should lynch and burn you the Ambassador of the African Republic in Africa will send home the news to Africa and we will send our battleships." If some said or sneered that "this is a dream," Garvey responded: "it wasn't a dream for George Washington."[20]

Nothing attracted more popular enthusiasm or brought more financial support from the UNIA faithful than did the Black Star Line. Even with three rickety, problem-plagued ships, it served as a symbol of power, pride, and destiny in a world of commerce and migration, and thousands of blacks turned out at ports from New York to Havana to Colón, Panama, to greet the Black Star vessels when they steamed in. "It must be understood," a federal agent could report in the fall of 1920, "that the foundation and strength of Garvey's anti-white movement rests solely on his retaining ownership of these ships . . . [whose] commercial value . . . is by far a secondary consideration against their moral and racial value."[21]

The popular appeal of the Black Star Line is wor-

thy of attention not because it identifies an entre-
preneurial and capitalistic impulse among Garvey's
followers or because it suggests the fundamentally
bourgeois orientation of the movement (though, of
course, these arguments can and have been made,
especially when Garveyism is viewed from the top
down);[22] it is worthy of attention because it draws us
to deeper currents of sensibility and practice, of aspiration and belief among many thousands of African Americans and thereby helps us understand how
Garvey was able to build a mass movement so
quickly, and one that would endure in many incarnations.

Garvey and other UNIA leaders attracted a mass
following because they cultivated fertile terrain. Together they offered a critique of American society
that made sense to black Americans. They spoke a
language that had familiar ideas and cadences. They
tapped into long-standing institutional forums and
rituals, especially those associated with churches and
fraternal societies. And they offered means and ends
that comported with grassroots struggles of the
postemancipation period and with the more general
social and political experience of most African Americans. They also constructed a global context that enabled followers to envision a new and expansive arena

Parade supporting the UNIA International Convention in New York City, 1920.

Courtesy of Photographs and Prints Division, Schomburg Center for Research in Black Culture, The New York Public Library, Astor, Lenox, and Tilden Foundations.

of strength, numbers, and power, and new and expansive identities based on categories and associations that had come to organize their lives, "race" chief among them. The problem is that these confluences have been greatly underappreciated.

To be sure, the intellectual genealogy of Garvey

and Garveyism has been elaborated before, and it includes a collection of nationalists, protonationalists,
and emigrationists of the nineteenth and early twentieth centuries: Martin Delany, Alexander Crummell,
Edward Blyden, Booker T. Washington, and Henry
McNeal Turner. It includes, as well, Pan-Africanists
like Duse Mohammed Ali, on whose paper, the *African Times and Orient Review,* Garvey worked when he
was in London during the early 1910s, and even
W. E. B. Du Bois, whose famed battles with Garvey
can easily obscure the perspectives they shared. Here
scholars have emphasized the embrace of Christian-
ity and European culture, the idea of "civilizing" Africa and Africans, and the need for self-help, uplift,
community development, and industrial education.
And there is much in Garvey's speeches and writings—particularly in his early speeches and writings,
that is to say, before he came to the United States—to
bear these lineages out.[23]

Yet what has often been overlooked—and at times
ignored—are the ways in which issues of self-
governance and separatism, rather than civilization-
ism and repatriation, enlivened Garvey's projects for
African Americans whose parents had been born into
slavery and who grew up, overwhelmingly, in the ru-

ral and small-town South of the late nineteenth century (which is to say that this was not a "back-to-Africa" movement). "I am proud of the fact that I am a member of what I consider the greatest organization in the world," a black North Carolinian wrote to the editor of the *Negro World* in 1925, adding, "I see nothing left for the Negro except to try to regain his motherland where he may *govern himself* and may have freedom for himself and the respect of other races and nations." The impulse to self-governance emerged out of the struggles and experiences of enslavement and quickly manifested itself in the period after emancipation. It was to be seen in the efforts of newly freed people to reconstitute their kinship groups, to form squads and other family-based work units, to pool community resources, and, of course, to acquire land. It was to be seen in the process of mobilizing Union Leagues and other paramilitary organizations during Reconstruction, in the battles over officeholding and policy influence in local Republican Parties, and in the forging of what were known as "fusion," or power-sharing, agreements with Democrats once Reconstruction collapsed. Indeed, instead of subsuming the impulse to self-governance to the larger quest for "citizenship," the two may better be seen as interconnected, perhaps mutually constituting.[24]

Self-governance and separatism were especially powerful in fueling a grassroots emigrationism that began to take shape immediately after emancipation and then developed into a large movement in the cotton belt of the Deep South during the 1870s and 1880s. In this pursuit, African Americans held local meetings, organized clubs, petitioned Congress and the president, corresponded with the American Colonization Society, circulated literature, and looked to a variety of sites—in the trans-Mississippi West, in the Caribbean, and in Liberia—not to do missionary work, not to civilize the "heathen," but rather to reestablish their communities on a more stable and secure footing. They spoke of escaping the threats, coercions, vulnerabilities, and limited prospects for themselves and their children, of "organising our selfs for homes," of establishing "for them selves and for the rising and future generation A free and independent government," of making "themselves a name and a nation." "[W]e wants to be a People," two leaders in Chickasaw County, Mississippi, proclaimed, "we cant be it heare and find that we ar compell to leve this Cuntry." So prophetic did the aspirations and goals seem that they were likened to an "exodus," and some of their participants were called "exodusters"; so contagious were the hopes and excitement that they were likened to a "fever."[25]

The obstacles that postemancipation emigrationists faced were formidable, to say the least. Their employers might try to block them by means of intimidation and violence, and some of their own political and religious leaders might attempt to dissuade them for fear of losing congregations and followings. Since most prospective emigrants imagined resettling in groups linked by kinship, religion, and labor, the challenges were both logistical and financial: accumulating the necessary resources, agreeing on a destination, making arrangements for transportation, and finding their way to rail stations and port cities—all in a context of severe economic stringency and an agricultural calendar that offered very few windows of opportunity for departure. Some black communities struggled heroically for years, to little avail. "You must Bar with us," one local emigrationist, with remarkable faith and determination, told the American Colonization Society after two years of saving "all the Money tha Could" to relocate in Liberia. "[T]he children of Israel was 40 years getting out

of the Williness and 25 or 35 are non to long for us."
Not surprisingly, few African Americans managed to
move out of the South during these years.[26]

But it does appear that a great many—perhaps a
great many more than we have yet recognized—found
other avenues to attain a semblance of these goals.
Some established colonies and what have come to be
called "black towns," sporadically during the period
of Reconstruction and then with more frequency between 1885 and 1905, as black entrepreneurs acquired
the necessary capital and connections and as the conditions of black life became increasingly intolerable.
Over twenty such towns would eventually be founded
in Oklahoma, but most of them grew up in parts of
the Deep South. A few, like Mound Bayou in Mississippi and Promiseland in South Carolina, have attracted scholarly and public notice; the greater number of them remained in the shadows, well beyond
the gaze of whites, with names often befitting their
purposes: Freetown, South Carolina; New Rising Star
and Klondike, Alabama; Peace and Bookman, Arkansas; and New Africa, Mississippi.[27]

Even so, many more African Americans came to
reside in unincorporated settlements, clustered on
tenant plantations or located at the edges of market
towns or growing around small hubs of black land-

owners and renters, that were held together by kinship groups, churches, schools, and benevolent societies and by a determination to distance themselves,
as far as possible, from the reach of whites. In east
Texas, more than five hundred such settlements came
into being between 1865 and 1900. Some were composed chiefly of sharecroppers and known to local
whites as Cocklebur, Fly Blow, and Niggertown. Others had their origins among black squatters who
struggled their way to landownership or among former slaves who were deeded land by their former
owners; their names derived from the creeks, hills, or
bottoms where they were located or from the praise
houses and chapels at which their denizens wor-
shiped. Still others took shape near urban places like
Austin, close enough for easy access to public work
yet distant enough to feel independent, and identified as Wheatsville, Horst's Pasture, Ryne Branch,
and Gregorytown.[28]

Many of these settlements survived well into the
twentieth century, and there is every reason to believe
that they had counterparts elsewhere in the South:
in the pine barrens of northern Florida and western
South Carolina, in southwest Georgia and the hills of
Alabama and Mississippi. Early in the twentieth century, several black families leased a hilltop just out-

side the Mississippi Delta that they chose to call the Place. There they not only grew cotton and corn but also took care of their subsistence needs as well as possible to keep white creditors at bay. Their relative success and cohesiveness were doubtless unusual in the rural South; the circumstances and impulses most certainly were not. This, after all, is what W. E. B. Du Bois discovered during his journey to southwest Georgia in the late 1890s and then wrote about so powerfully in *The Souls of Black Folk*. In Dougherty County he came upon the "hundred cabin homes" surrounding Shepherd's Church, where, he learned, on a Sunday five hundred worshippers would gather "to talk and eat and sing." He found, too, a schoolhouse nearby and next to it a two-story lodge where "societies to care for the sick and bury the dead would meet," societies that, even in this "forlorn and forsaken" part of the South, "grow and flourish."[29]

Amid the violent white supremacist campaigns of the late nineteenth and early twentieth centuries, which sought to enforce black submission through lynching, disfranchisement, and legal segregation, distance, numbers, and arms offered the best protections—as they always had. Under these precarious circumstances, who could deny Garvey's claim that

America was a white man's country, that white racism was intractable, that white allies were few and ineffective, and that blacks had to organize for self-defense? And as black soldiers returned from a war to make the "world safe for democracy" only to find a hardened and more vicious Jim Crow at home, as thousands of black southerners made their way into the cities of the North, and as black newspapers like the *Chicago Defender* and then the *Negro World* began to circulate North and South, apprising African Americans of a wide and complex world, who could not be energized by Garvey's vision of 400 million black allies over the globe?

⚬⚬⚬

The extent of UNIA organizing and appeal in any section of the United States is, at the present time, barely understood. The locations of the many divisions established in the 1910s and 1920s offer a useful starting point, but they may also direct us to a significant underground of African American political activity in the nineteenth and twentieth centuries of which the UNIA was only a part. UNIA divisions in the South, for example, tended to surface in areas—southeast Virginia, eastern North Carolina, southwest Georgia, Louisiana, the Arkansas-Mississippi

Delta—where emigrationist sentiment had developed four decades earlier and then carved arenas of social and political activism. Emigrationists of the 1870s, 1880s, and 1890s, in turn, carried their sensibilities with them if and when they migrated from southeast to southwest (to newly cleared and drained lands of Arkansas, Missouri, Louisiana, and Texas), from countryside to town (the first moves of what turned into the Great Migration), and eventually from South to North. The earliest UNIA mobilizations in the southern states occurred in Hampton Roads, Newport News, Norfolk, and Portsmouth, Virginia, where emigrationism had long been in evidence and from which American Colonization Society vessels had long departed for Liberia—and to which families (like that of the civil rights leader Ella Baker) moved from eastern and east-central North Carolina, where emigrationism was especially widespread. Still other Garveyites had been among the estimated 300,000 African Americans who became involved in the National Ex-Slave Mutual Relief, Bounty, and Pension Association—what can be regarded as the first mass reparations movement—established around the turn of the twentieth century by a Tennessean, Callie House, herself a washerwoman and former slave.[30]

Organized chiefly in the late 1910s and early 1920s,

UNIA divisions in the South appear to have held on long after the movement crested and Marcus Garvey had come under intense fire. In the period between 1926 and 1928, over four hundred divisions were operating in the southern states, and by that point Garvey had been indicted, tried, convicted, and incarcerated, and he was on the verge of deportation. Little is known about the subsequent histories of these divisions, though in all likelihood their members found outlets for their political energies if their divisions became moribund. In eastern Arkansas, counties that had a substantial UNIA presence in the 1920s became bases for the Southern Tenant Farmers Union (STFU) in the 1930s; in the 1940s and 1950s some of the STFU faithful became active in local struggles for civil rights.[31]

The Arkansas-Mississippi Delta not only proved to be fertile ground for the UNIA; it also sprouted chapters of the NAACP, particularly after the Elaine Massacre of 1919, when planters brutally crushed the Progressive Farmers and Household Union, which had been contemplating a strike. The NAACP is, of course, associated with the legalistic road of the Civil Rights movement, and its base has been seen to be among the urban black middle and professional classes. For the most part, this appears to be true.

Application and membership records show that law-yers, physicians, ministers, teachers, and government employees were prominent, especially in the larger towns and cities of the South. (See table 5 in the appendix.) Yet, in the late 1910s and early 1920s, the NAACP cast an even wider net, moving—often at the behest of local activists—into small towns and vil-lages and attracting (in town and country) laborers, farmers, seamstresses, laundresses, letter carriers, jan-itors, and dock workers. By 1921 the NAACP had Ken-tucky branches in Cynthiana, Earlington, Maysville, and Hopkinsville, as well as in Louisville, Lexington, and Frankfort; had Georgia branches in Waycross, Thomasville, Brunswick, and Rome, as well as in At-lanta, Savannah, and Macon; and had Texas branches in Wharton, Orange, Corsicana, and Texarkana, as well as in Houston, Galveston, and Dallas.[32]

Although branch directors (including James Weldon Johnson) for the NAACP kept files on the activities of Garvey and the UNIA, and although Garvey tangled with and denounced the work of the NAACP, closer to the ground the organizations seem not to have competed for members—at least outside the large cit-ies. In Kentucky the UNIA had divisions in places like Banham, Coxton, Erlander, and Sassafras; in Georgia in places like Camilla, Haylow, Shingler, and Ty Ty; in

Texas in places like Cameron, Egypt, Hillsboro, and Whitney—and some of these, barely recognizable and almost impossible to find on a map, may well have been unincorporated settlements.[33]

Where the NAACP and UNIA overlapped, their organizational histories may have been sequential and members may have moved between them. This appears to have been the case in the Mississippi Delta town of Caruthersville, Missouri. A thriving commercial center in what is known as the bootheel section of the state, Caruthersville had become a magnet for rural wage workers; by 1920 the town had a population of over 1,100 African Americans, including petty professionals and merchants. That same year the NAACP established a chapter with nearly 70 members representing something of a cross section of the community. Within two years the chapter was on the verge of collapse, but the UNIA had started to grow in the area on a base of black tenants who were relatively longtime residents, stable financially, and older family heads: very much the profile of Garveyites elsewhere in the South. By 1924, 14 UNIA divisions had been established in Missouri's bootheel, bolstered by a large influx of black laborers who may already have been exposed to Garvey and the UNIA in Mississippi or Arkansas. But the institutional shift could also be in the opposite direction. Thus, in East Drew, Mississippi, a local minister who served as a UNIA secretary in the 1920s went on to affiliate himself with the NAACP in the late 1930s—a path later followed by E. D. Nixon, who helped organize the Montgomery bus boycott.[34]

The Jim Crow South therefore not only included vibrant African American political thoroughfares, many effectively subterranean; it also evinced a hybridity of politics and political ideas among African Americans that defies the customary oppositions of integrationism and separatism, assimilationism and nationalism, NAACP and UNIA, civil rights and black power.[35] These thoroughfares and this hybridity help us better understand how interconnected and mutually reinforcing black political trajectories have been in the last century, and how important—especially among workers and the poor—have been traditions of self-governance and self-defense.[36]

Indeed, we may gain a far deeper sense of the development of movements such as the very broadly conceived "Black Power," which are now attracting a good deal of scholarly interest yet are seen, chiefly, as phenomena of the period after World War II. The history of the UNIA, of Garveyites, and of Garveyism during the 1930s, 1940s, and 1950s—of Garvey-

ism after Garvey—may offer crucial clues to the organizational and intellectual foundations of a variety
of cultural and political mobilizations (from the Nation of Islam to the Organization of African Unity
to the Revolutionary Action Movement to the Black
Panther Party), as well as to the reshaping of early
twentieth-century nationalism and Pan-Africanism
in the face of world war and decolonization.

UNIA divisions, at least those outside New York,
always had a good deal of local autonomy, and although there were significant membership declines
and serious organizational ruptures during the Depression, the UNIA survived in a variety of forms. In
some cases, powerful leaders like Captain A. L. King
in New York kept large divisions afloat; in other
cases, as in the Detroit area, smaller divisions were
consolidated. John Vincent, who served as an officer in Hamtramck Division No. 159, which had between 150 and 200 members, recalled that when regular meetings had to be discontinued during the 1930s
owing to the strains of renting a hall, he and his fellow Garveyites went "down to the Detroit Division
and ma[d]e one big division." At all events, community ties were renewed and reinvigorated as the UNIA
set up youth groups, operated businesses, provided
food and clothing to those in need, paid for burials,

and helped fight battles over housing and employment. In Virginia some Garveyites formed the Negro Political Union and urged blacks to pay the poll tax and qualify for voting, while others involved themselves with boycotts or cooperatives. Where the UNIA disbanded entirely, former supporters often continued their community-based activities (many became involved in the "Don't Buy Where You Can't Work" campaigns of the 1930s) or gravitated to any one of several organizations: the Communist and Socialist parties, the Future Outlook League, the CIO, the AFL, or the Brotherhood of Sleeping Car Porters.[37]

The Nation of Islam, especially in the urban Midwest, recruited many men and women who had been drawn to and influenced by Garvey and Garveyism, and their social profiles were much like Elijah Muhammad's, himself associated with the UNIA when he was in Chicago. They tended to be over thirty years of age and migrants from rural areas of the South. But the evidence, limited as it still is, suggests more than discrete new pathways; it also suggests movements and coalitions involving a number of organizations. The career and activities of Charlotta Bass illuminate these dimensions. Born in Sumter, South Carolina, around 1880, Bass moved to Rhode Island after finishing high school and began working in the newspaper business. In 1910, partly on the advice of her doctor, she migrated to Los Angeles, where she sold newspaper subscriptions before taking over as the editor of the *California Eagle* around 1912, an increasingly important African American paper whose readership would reach nearly 18,000 by the 1940s. A lifelong political activist perhaps best known for her battles against racially restrictive covenants, Bass in the 1920s held memberships simultaneously in the UNIA and the NAACP; she regularly promoted the programs and undertakings of both in the pages of the *Eagle*. It was a pattern of institutional fluidity that would continue to mark African American politics in Los Angeles even after the UNIA faded, as chapters of the NAACP, CORE, and the Nation of Islam cooperated in local struggles and carried forward the discourse of political and cultural nationalism. Bass herself ran for the Los Angeles City Council and then for Congress, was nominated for the vice presidency by Paul Robeson at the 1952 Progressive Party national convention, and remained involved with issues of fair housing, economic empowerment, voter registration, prisoners' rights, and South African apartheid until her death in 1969.[38]

Many other African Americans whose lives spanned the first two-thirds of the twentieth century had political sensibilities and journeys that resembled those of Charlotta Bass. Sylvia Woods grew up in New Orleans and attended UNIA meetings with her father, a local labor activist. There she not only delighted in the pageantry and music at Longshoreman's Hall; she was also riveted by a woman who used to speak powerfully "every Sunday." Woods's affiliations would later include the Communist Party, the CIO, and the Free Angela Davis Committee. In 1946 she became the first African American woman to run for the Illinois General Assembly. Like Woods, Randolph Blackwell was introduced to Marcus Garvey and the UNIA by his father, though the Blackwells resided in Greensboro, North Carolina. Blackwell sold the *Negro World* locally and remained a UNIA loyalist into the 1930s, when he and his father moved toward the NAACP. He eventually worked with the Southern Christian Leadership Council and the Voter Education Project in North Carolina, but he always valued the UNIA's interest in organizing the "masses."[39]

James Anderson of the small Delta town of Camden, Arkansas, embraced the UNIA with the enthusiasm of Woods and Blackwell, but he could not bring himself to embrace the NAACP because Du Bois "seemed to oppose Marcus Garvey's program and I was on Garvey's side." Impressed by its support of the Scottsboro boys, Anderson briefly considered joining the Communist Party, though he "came to the conclusion that their economic system was too harsh." Moving to Chicago in the mid-1930s, he instead was attracted to the Nation of Islam, in which, as James X, he became an assistant minister of the Chicago mosque and an adviser to Elijah Muhammad. A native of New Orleans, Queen Mother Audley Moore participated actively in the UNIA during the early 1920s and, by her own telling, had her political consciousness shaped for her entire life. Over the next four decades, Moore aligned with the Communist Party, the Revolutionary Action Movement, and the Republic of New Africa, and in 1950 she organized the Universal Association of Ethiopian Women, which concerned itself with welfare rights, anti-lynching legislation, and prisoners' rights. "Marcus Garvey," she later declared, "raised me in a certain knowledge of me belonging to people all over the world, the African people, and he gave me pride."[40]

No one better exemplified the extended genealogies of Garveyism and Black Power than did Malcolm X. We are, of course, well aware of Malcolm's enormous influence on the development of nationalist and Pan-Africanist thought in the second half of the twentieth century, and certainly on the education of young black militants in organizations such as RAM (Revolutionary Action Movement), DRUM (Dodge Revolutionary Union Movement), US, and the Black Panthers. Yet less notice is taken of the intellectual and political legacies that Malcolm himself enlivened. His father, Earl Little, born in rural Georgia, was a Garveyite from his days in Omaha, Nebraska, and went on to become active in Lansing, Michigan, before he was killed under suspicious circumstances, which helps us understand Malcolm's prison embrace of the Nation of Islam. As early as 1954, when Malcolm took charge of Mosque No. 7 in Harlem, he forged close ties with Lewis Michaux, an old Garveyite whose bookstore became the site of Malcolm's outdoor rallies. When Malcolm ultimately traveled to Ghana and met President Kwame Nkrumah, who had been educated in the United States and was deeply affected by Garvey's thought, an Atlantic world of Garveyism seemed symbolically reunited. "Every time you see another nation on the African continent become independent," Malcolm X could tell an interviewer several months before his own death, "you know that Marcus Garvey is alive. It was Marcus Garvey's philosophy of Pan Africanism that initiated the entire freedom movement . . . and had it not been for Marcus Garvey, and the foundations laid by him, you would find no independent nations in the Caribbean today. All the freedom movements that are taking place right here in America today were initiated by the work and teachings of Marcus Garvey."[41]

࿐

Why is it that we know so little of these genealogies? Why is it that this grassroots political history remains largely hidden from our view? In part it is because of the ways in which local black activists—especially those associated with the UNIA—practiced their politics and set their political goals. Outside the cities, UNIA divisions had relatively few members (mostly fewer than fifty); they could meet in lodges, farmhouses, and churches without attracting very much attention; and they generally did not stage processions and parades. They also did not seek to challenge the Jim Crow system directly and thereby did not pose any recognized threat to local whites. Although any black assemblies could court white harassment, and word of the UNIA's presence could strike alarm among whites, little notice of the UNIA was registered in the public record.[42] Not so with the NAACP, which required fifty members for a charter, was a known enemy of Jim Crow, and struggled (often unsuccessfully in the South) to survive. So we have to look hard. Why, given the size and scope of the movement, haven't we?

The declining interest in social historical work and methods has played a role in keeping this political world hidden from our view. Despite the limitations of the public record, we could learn a great deal about the character of the UNIA in different parts of the country from sources that are readily available. But that would require copying down lots of names, referencing them in census and tax records, trying to follow them over time and space, and tracing the circuits of correspondence and information. And few historians seem inclined to do this sort of thing—even though changing technologies have made it a great deal more manageable than it once was. Predictably, recent scholarship that touches on Garvey and the UNIA focuses either on the discourse and its imagined middle-class constituency or on the leadership and the leading critics.[43]

Yet what has kept this world hidden has far less to do with methodological preferences, and far more to do with intellectual and political indispositions. Historians and other writers have not been much interested in Marcus Garvey, in the UNIA movement, in the sort of people who gravitated to the movement, or in the current of nationalist thinking that Garveyism represented.[44] They have, on the other hand, been very much interested in W. E. B. Du Bois and the legacies with which he is identified. And although Du Bois admired Garvey's charisma, energy, and eloquence, he not only attacked Garvey's politics and behavior but also helped isolate Garvey in the midst of his legal woes. Du Bois described Garvey as a "stubborn and domineering leader," as an "inexperienced business man," and as a "demagogue" whose "movement is not representative of the American negro," but whose "followers are of the lowest types of negroes, mostly from the Indies." In Du Bois's view, Garvey's projects were "dangerous, ill-considered, impractical," and bordering on the "criminal." The UNIA, Du Bois declared, "cannot be considered an American movement in any sense of the word." This portrait, and these charges, have been adopted by many historians, and they have helped discourage scholars from taking Garvey and the UNIA seriously.[45]

But the embrace of Du Bois and the disparagement of Garvey may reflect a far broader and deeper phenomenon: the powerful influence that a liberal integrationist framework and narrative have had on American history writing for at least the past half

century. Whether exploring the mid-eighteenth century, when the slave population of British North
America began to reproduce itself; or the antebellum
period, when free blacks in the North began to mobi-
lize for their safety and their rights; or the era of
emancipation and Reconstruction, when freed people began to organize in new ways; or the twentieth-
century battles against Jim Crow, historians have
tended to develop their approaches and analyses
around a widely accepted set of ideas. They have emphasized African American identification with the
United States and have diminished the importance
of black interest in emigration, repatriation, or Pan-
Africanism. They have considered slaves to be apoliti-
cal or "pre-political" people, capable of resistance or
even rebellion but unable to constitute themselves
as political actors in any recognizable way, and they
therefore have seen "politics" coming to ex-slaves from
outside their own communities. They have privileged
and lent legitimacy to African American struggles for
inclusion and assimilation, for individual rights, and
for citizenship, while at the same time regarding African American interest in separatism and community
development, in collective rights, and in forms of nationalism as the products of failure and defeat, as
somehow lacking in integrity. Voices and movements

that do not fit the integrationist framework or narrative tend to be either ignored or relegated to the margins, acknowledged only to be diminished in significance, viewed chiefly as components of the pathologies and cycles of American racism. And although a growing number of historians have offered significant challenges to this perspective, they have not yet threatened to displace it.[46]

Not surprisingly, many of the major historical works on Marcus Garvey and the UNIA have been produced by scholars born and educated in the Caribbean and Britain rather than in the United States: Robert Hill, Tony Martin, Rupert Lewis, Winston James, and, most recently, Colin Grant. They have certainly begun to excavate a political history that has long been hidden and have laid a scholarly foundation that is formidable and immensely valuable. But their work needs to be continued, their leads pursued. Garvey and the UNIA electrified black America during the 1920s and, in so doing, provided for what may well have been the first great moment of African American political and racial consciousness that was truly national in scope: a language, a worldview, a critical perspective, a set of goals, and a sense of destiny that could be shared by people of African descent in the United States whether they lived in

New York or Los Angeles, Miami or Chicago, New Orleans or Oakland, Merigold (Miss.) or Kalamazoo (Mich.), Buxton (Iowa) or Camilla (Ga.), Cotton Plant (Ark.) or Egg Harbor (N.J.), Biggs (Okla.) or Victorville (Calif.). In looking well beyond the borders of the United States—to Canada, the Caribbean, Central America, South America, southern and western Africa—Garvey and the UNIA, aided by the international circulation of the *Negro World,* also electrified much of the black Atlantic world and created what may well have been one of the great movements of diasporic peoples in modern history. Given the thousands, if not millions, of people of African descent who came within the orbit of Garveyism, who regarded themselves as Garveyites, and who transmitted their experiences and sensibilities to subsequent generations, in some cases with stunning political results, we condescend to Garvey and the UNIA at our own loss and our own peril.

APPENDIX

NOTES

ACKNOWLEDGMENTS

INDEX

APPENDIX

The following tables, which provide social and demographic profiles of African Americans who joined or supported Marcus Garvey's Universal Negro Improvement Association, were compiled from lists of nearly 3,400 individuals who contributed money to the organization (usually ranging from five to twenty-five cents) sometime in 1923. Their names and places of residence were printed in the pages of the *Negro World* during that year. I tried to discover as much as I could about these individuals—their birthplaces, their ages, their occupations and property ownership, their genders and marital status, and their literacy—and, to that end, attempted to locate as many as possible in the population schedules of the Federal Manuscript Census for 1920 (the decennial census closest to 1923). The task was made especially difficult because of the three-year discrepancy between the time the census was taken and the time the names appeared in the *Negro World* (many had shifted their residence), because many of the names included only initials rather than full first names, and because many of the Garveyites from small towns and rural areas (North, South, and West) lived either in unincorporated townships and districts or in places that were not identified by the census takers.

Ultimately, I found about four hundred of the Garveyites, although their distribution by gender and region was quite similar to the larger group as a whole. Table 5, which compares UNIA supporters with NAACP members in Baton Rouge, Louisiana, also depended on information in the NAACP Branch Files, housed in the Library of Congress in Washington, D.C. My general knowledge about the number and geographical distribution of UNIA divisions owes much both to the Records of the UNIA Central Division, held in the Schomburg Center for Research in Black Culture in New York City, and to the multivolume *Marcus Garvey and Universal Negro Improvement Association Papers,* edited by Robert A. Hill and his colleagues and published by the University of California Press.

Table 1 UNIA divisions and supporters by region, 1920s

Region	Divisions		Supporters	
	N	%	N	%
Northeast	165	17.6	784	23.2
Midwest	241	25.7	579	17.1
South	482	51.5	1,853	54.8
West	48	5.1	166	4.9
Totals*	936	99.9	3,382	100.0

Sources: Negro World, 1923; Robert A. Hill et al., eds., *The Marcus Garvey and Universal Negro Improvement Association Papers,* 10 vols. (Berkeley, Calif.: 1983–2006), 7:986–1002.

   *Percentage may not add up to 100.0 because of rounding.

Table 2 Birthplaces of UNIA supporters, 1923

Residence of supporters	State of residence	State in North	Place of birth State in South	Caribbean/ Canada	No.
Urban North[a]	8.2%	1.5%	71.7%	18.6%	194
Urban South[b]	62.8%	1.2%	32.1%	3.9%	78
Rural/small town North[c]	—	—	100.0%	—	6
Rural/small town South[d]	74.0%	—	26.0%	—	114

Sources: Negro World, 1923; United States Census, Schedule of Population, 1920, National Archives, Washington, D.C.

[a] Includes supporters from Boston, Chicago, Cincinnati, Cleveland, Dayton, Detroit, Gary, Hartford, Indianapolis, Jersey City, Manhattan, Albany, Philadelphia, and Pittsburgh.

[b] Includes supporters from Bacon Rouge, New Orleans, Washington, D.C., Wilmington, Del, Miami, Atlanta, Macon, Ga, and Richmond.

[c] Includes supporters from Santoy (Bearfield), Ohio.

[d] Includes supporters from Amorel, Ark.; Bayou Goula, La.; Dewitt, Va.; Humboldt, Tenn.; La Place, La.; Magnolia, N.C.; Merigold, Miss.; Sumner, Miss.; Madison, Ark.; Round Pond, Ark.; Plaquemine, La.; New Madrid, Mo.; Boley, Okla.; Guthrie, Okla.; Suffolk, Va.; Monongah, W.Va.; Maysville, S.C.

Table 3   Occupations of UNIA supporters, 1923

I. Urban occupations

	North		South	
	N	%	N	%
Professional	5	2.7	3	3.9
Supervisor	3	1.6	2	2.6
White collar	3	1.6	2	2.6
Commerce and retail	2	1.1	3	3.9
Service	43	22.9	17	22.1
Transportation	11	5.9	7	9.1
Skilled or semiskilled worker	86	45.7	21	27.3
Laborer	33	17.6	18	23.4
Other	2	1.1	4	5.1
Totals*	188	100.2	77	100.0

II. Small town and rural occupations

	North		South	
	N	%	N	%
Farm owner	—	—	19	17.1
Farm tenant	—	—	33	29.7
Commerce and retail	—	—	2	1.8
Service	—	—	6	5.4
Transportation	—	—	2	1.8
Skilled or semiskilled worker	6	100.0	25	22.5
Farm laborer	—	—	24	21.6
Totals*	6	100.0	111	99.9

Sources: Negro World, 1923; United States Census, Schedule of Population, 1920.

*Percentages may not add up to 100.0 because of rounding.

Table 4   Gender, average age, and marital status of UNIA supporters, 1923

	North		South	
	N	%	N	%
Male	141	69.5	145	74.7
Female	62	30.5	49	25.3
Married	149	75.3	155	80.7
Widowed	17	8.6	16	8.3
Unmarried	32	16.2	21	10.9
Average age				
Male	41.1		42.1	
Female	36.0		41.1	

Sources: Negro World, 1923; United States Census, Schedule of Population, 1920.

Table 5   Occupations of UNIA supporters and NAACP
members, Baton Rouge, Louisiana, 1919–1923

Occupation	UNIA (%) N = 12	NAACP (%) N = 59
Professional	—	6.7
Religious	—	5.1
Education	8.3	5.1
Retail	—	8.5
Government work	—	1.7
Farmer or tenant	8.3	3.4
Skilled or semiskilled worker	33.3	54.2
Laborer	50.0	15.3
Total*	99.9	100.0

Sources: Papers of the National Association for the Advancement of
Colored People, Branch Files, Baton Rouge, La., 1919, 12A, Roll 13,
Library of Congress, Washington, D.C.; *Negro World,* 1923; United States
Census, Schedule of Population, 1920.

   *Percentage may not add up to 100.0 because of rounding.

Notes

1. "Slaves at Large"

1. Lewis Garrard Clarke, *Narrative of the Sufferings of Lewis Clarke, During a Captivity of More than Twenty-five Years, Among the Algerines of Kentucky, One of the So Called Christian States of North America* (Boston, 1845), 35–38, 42 (emphasis in original).

2. Moses Roper, *A Narrative of the Adventures and Escape of Moses Roper, from American Slavery* (Philadelphia, 1838), 76–84; Thomas Smallwood, *A Narrative of Thomas Smallwood (Coloured Man) . . . Written by Himself* (Toronto, 1851), 44–46 (emphasis in original). Also see Frederick Douglass, *My Bondage and My Freedom,* ed. William L. Andrews (1855; rept., Urbana, Ill., 1987), 206; Henry Box Brown and Charles Stearns, *Narrative of Henry Box Brown* (Boston, 1849), 65; William Wells Brown, *Narrative of William Wells Brown, a Fugitive Slave* (Boston, 1847), 105, 110; Josiah Henson, *The Life of Josiah Henson, Formerly a Slave, Now an Inhabitant of Canada, as Narrated by Himself* (Boston, 1849), 48; James W. C. Pennington,

The Fugitive Blacksmith . . . Formerly a Slave in the State of Maryland (London, 1849), 51–52.

3. Arthur Zilversmit, *The First Emancipation: The Abolition of Slavery in the North* (Chicago, 1967).

4. For more on this comparison, see chapter 2.

5. See Lorenzo Greene, *The Negro in Colonial New England* (New York, 1942); Ira Berlin, *Many Thousands Gone: The First Two Centuries of Slavery in North America* (Cambridge, Mass., 1998); Joanne Pope Melish, *Disowning Slavery: Gradual Emancipation and "Race" in New England, 1780–1860* (Ithaca, 1998); Gary Nash, *Forging Freedom: The Formation of Philadelphia's Black Community, 1720–1840* (Cambridge, Mass., 1988); Shane White, *Somewhat More Independent: The End of Slavery in New York City, 1770–1810* (Athens, Ga., 1991); Graham Russell Hodges, *Slavery and Freedom in the Rural North: African Americans in Monmouth County, New Jersey, 1665–1865* (Madison, Wisc., 1997); Leslie M. Harris, *In the Shadow of Slavery: African Americans in New York City, 1626–1863* (Chicago, 2003); James Oliver Horton and Lois E. Horton, *In Hope of Liberty: Culture, Community, and Protest among Northern Free Blacks, 1700–1860* (New York, 1997); Jill Lepore, *New York Burning: Liberty, Slavery, and Conspiracy in Eighteenth-Century Manhattan* (New York, 2005); John Wood Sweet, *Bodies Politic: Negotiating Race in the American North, 1730–1830* (Baltimore, 2003), 4, 60–62.

6. Zilversmit, *First Emancipation,* 109–200; Berlin, *Many Thousands Gone,* 228–55; Gary B. Nash and Jean R. Soderlund, *Freedom by Degrees: Emancipation in Pennsylvania and Its Aftermath* (New York, 1991); Melish, *Disowning Slavery,* 50–83; Donald Robinson, *Slavery in the Structure of American Politics, 1765–1820* (New York, 1971), 22–38; David Brion Davis, *The Problem of Slavery in the Age of Revolution, 1770–1823* (Ithaca, 1975), 86–89; Leon Litwack, *North of Slavery: The Negro in the Free States* (Chicago, 1961), 3–29.

7. Zilversmit, *First Emancipation,* 116–17, 201–29; White, *Somewhat More Independent,* 24–55; Hodges, *Slavery and Freedom in the Rural North,* 175. The New Jersey legislation, as Hodges points out, turned the state's remaining slaves into "lifetime apprentices" and did not free any of the state's remaining seven hundred slaves. By "people officially acknowledged as slaves," I mean those recorded as slaves in the census and other official records. I do not mean those who were fugitives from states where slavery remained legal and who, owing to the Fugitive Slave Laws, carried the status of slave into states where slavery, at least in theory, was illegal. I will develop this point later in the chapter.

8. Ira Berlin, *Slaves without Masters: The Free Negro in the Antebellum South* (New York, 1974), 15–78, 135–38.

9. William W. Freehling, *The Road to Disunion: The Secessionists at Bay, 1776–1854* (New York, 1990), 162–96;

Alison Goodyear-Freehling, *Drift toward Dissolution: The Virginia Slavery Debate of 1831–1832* (Baton Rouge, 1982).

10. The Northwest Ordinance is widely regarded as the most important piece of legislation enacted by Congress under the auspices of the Articles of Confederation. It laid explicit claim to the territory north and west of the Ohio River and provided a framework for bringing new states into the Union. Its wording on the issue of slavery would also be included in the Thirteenth Amendment to the Constitution.

11. Don E. Fehrenbacher, *The Slaveholding Republic: An Account of the United States Government's Relations to Slavery* (New York, 2001), 253–63; Paul Finkelman, "Evading the Ordinance: The Persistence of Bondage in Indiana and Illinois," *Journal of the Early Republic* 6 (Winter 1986): 343–70; Robert J. Steinfeld, *The Invention of Free Labor: The Employment Relation in English and American Law and Culture, 1350–1870* (Chapel Hill, 1991), 122–42; Eugene H. Berwanger, *The Frontier against Slavery: Western Anti-Negro Sentiment and the Slavery Extension Controversy* (Urbana, Ill., 1967), 7–29; Stephen Middleton, "The Fugitive Slave Crisis in Cincinnati, 1850–1860: Resistance, Enforcement, and Black Refugees," *Journal of Negro History* 72 (January 1987): 21; Christopher M. Osborne, "Invisible Hands: Slaves, Bound Laborers,

and the Development of Western Pennsylvania, 1780-1820," *Pennsylvania History* 72 (January 2005): 77-99; William Miller, "The Effects of the American Revolution on Indentured Servitude," *Pennsylvania History* 7 (July 1940): 131-41. Robert Steinfeld offers a particularly valuable and illuminating discussion of the changing relation between slavery and indentured servitude during the eighteenth and early nineteenth centuries.

12. Fehrenbacher, *Slaveholding Republic,* 205-30; Thomas D. Morris, *Free Men All: The Personal Liberty Laws of the North, 1780–1861* (Baltimore, 1974), 94-106; Joseph Nogee, "The Prigg Case and Fugitive Slavery, 1842-1850," *Journal of Negro History* 39 (July 1954): 185-205; Stanley W. Campbell, *The Slave Catchers: Enforcement of the Fugitive Slave Law, 1850–1860* (New York, 1972), 3-25; Don E. Fehrenbacher, *The Dred Scott Case: Its Significance in American Law and Politics* (New York, 1978); Paul Finkleman, *An Imperfect Union: Slavery, Federalism, and Comity* (Chapel Hill, 1981).

13. The most powerful statement along these lines, though not one that confronts the dynamics of the emancipation process, is Fehrenbacher, *Slaveholding Republic.* See also Steven Hahn, "Class and State in Postemancipation Societies: Southern Planters in Comparative Perspective," *American Historical Review* 95 (February 1990): 75-98.

14. On this point, see C. A. Bayly, *The Birth of the Modern*

World, 1780–1914 (Oxford, 2004), 247–83. It is worth noting that the century of slave emancipation in the Atlantic world (1780–1888) coincided with the century of peasant emancipations in continental Europe, what the historian Jerome Blum calls "the servile lands." And there, too, the emancipationist impulse often reflected the developing state's struggle for direct authority over the population within its territory as well as for access to the bodies of its subjects, especially for the purposes of military conscription. The best overall treatment is to be found in Jerome Blum, *The End of the Old Order in Rural Europe* (Princeton, 1978). For studies that link slave emancipation with the crisis of the colonial state, see Robin Blackburn, *The Overthrow of Colonial Slavery, 1776–1848* (London, 1988); and Christopher Leslie Brown, *Moral Capital: Foundations of British Abolitionism* (Chapel Hill, 2006).

15. On the problems that slavery and slaveholding posed for the new Confederate state, see Stephanie McCurry, *Confederate Crucible: The Unfranchised and Political Transformation of the Civil War South* (Cambridge, Mass., forthcoming); and Bruce Levine, *Confederate Emancipation: Southern Plans to Free and Arm Slaves during the Civil War* (New York, 2006).

16. See, for example, Charles Sellers, *The Market Revolution: Jacksonian America, 1815–1846* (New York, 1991); Melvyn Stokes and Stephen Conway, eds., *The Mar-*

ket Revolution in America: Social, Political, and Religious Expressions, 1800–1880 (Charlottesville, Va., 1996); Paul E. Johnson and Sean Wilentz, The Kingdom of Matthias: A Story of Sex and Salvation in Nineteenth Century America (New York, 1994); James R. Sharp, The Jacksonians versus the Banks: Politics in the States after the Panic of 1837 (New York, 1970); John Ashworth, "Agrarians" and "Aristocrats": Party Political Ideology in the United States, 1837–1846 (New York, 1987); Sean Wilentz, The Rise of American Democracy: Jefferson to Lincoln (New York, 2005), 533–39; Thomas Summerhill, "Anti-Abolitionist Rioting and the Secession Crisis in Syracuse, New York" (unpublished paper presented at the Conference on New York State History, Saratoga Springs, June 2007); Howard C. Perkins, "The Defense of Slavery in the Northern Press on the Eve of the Civil War," Journal of Southern History 9 (November 1943): 501–31; Iver Bernstein, The New York City Draft Riots: Their Significance for American Society and Politics in the Age of the Civil War (New York, 1990); Grace Palladino, Another Civil War: Labor, Capital, and the State in the Anthracite Regions of Pennsylvania, 1840–1868 (Urbana, Ill., 1990). On the sympathies of northern merchants and cotton manufacturers for the interests of southern slaveholders, see Thomas O'Connor, Lords of the Loom: The Cotton Whigs and the Coming of the Civil War (New York, 1968).

17. This is certainly true of James M. McPherson, *Battle Cry of Freedom: The Civil War Era* (New York, 1988), and Eric Foner, *Reconstruction: America's Unfinished Revolution, 1863–1877* (New York, 1988), still the two dominant treatments. For some attempts, limited though they are, to incorporate the trans-Mississippi West, see Alvin M. Josephy, *The Civil War in the American West* (New York, 1991); David A. Nichols, *Lincoln and the Indians: Civil War Policy and Politics* (Urbana, Ill., 1978); Michael Fellman, *Inside War: The Guerrilla Conflict in Missouri during the American Civil War* (New York, 1990); T. J. Stiles, *Jesse James: The Last Rebel of the Civil War* (New York, 2002); Heather Cox Richardson, *West from Appomattox: The Reconstruction of America after the Civil War* (New Haven, 2007); Robert R. Dykstra, *Bright Radical Star: Black Freedom and White Supremacy in the Hawkeye State* (Cambridge, Mass., 1993).

18. Steven Hahn, "Emancipation and the Development of Capitalist Agriculture: The South in Comparative Perspective," in *What Made the South Different?* ed. Kees Gispen (Jackson, Miss., 1990), 71–88; Howard Lamar, "From Bondage to Contract: Ethnic Labor in the American West, 1600–1890," in *The Countryside in the Age of Capitalist Transformation: Essays in the Social History of Rural America,* ed. Steven Hahn and Jonathan Prude (Chapel Hill, 1985), 293–324; Gunther Peck, *Reinventing Free Labor: Padrones*

and Immigrant Workers in the North American West,
1880–1930 (New York, 2000).

19. On contract and indentured laborers in the
postemancipation Americas, see David Northrup,
Indentured Labor in the Age of Imperialism, 1834–1922
(Cambridge, U.K., 1995); Walter Rodney, *A History of*
the Guyanese Working People, 1881–1905 (Baltimore,
1981), 31–59; Moon-Ho Jung, *Coolies and Cane: Race,*
Labor, and Sugar in the Age of Emancipation (Balti-
more, 2006); Alan Adamson, "The Reconstruction
of Plantation Life after Emancipation: The Case of
British Guiana," in *Race and Slavery in the Western*
Hemisphere: Quantitative Studies, ed. Eugene D.
Genovese and Stanley L. Engerman (Princeton,
1975), 457–73; Stanley L. Engerman, "Servants to
Slaves to Servants: Contract Labour and European
Expansion," in *Colonialism and Migration: Indentured*
Labour before and after Slavery, ed. P. C. Emmer
(Dordrecht, 1986), 270–76; William A. Green, *British*
Slave Emancipation: The Sugar Colonies and the Great
Experiment, 1830–1865 (Oxford, 1965), 192–218;
Thomas H. Holloway, *Immigrants on the Land: Coffee*
and Society in São Paulo, 1886–1934 (Chapel Hill, 1980);
Rebecca J. Scott, *Slave Emancipation in Cuba: The*
Transition to Free Labor (Princeton, 1985), 3–41, 63–
226; Hahn, "Emancipation and Development of
Capitalist Agriculture," 76–77.

20. For the important comparative works that focus on

the "second emancipation," often to the exclusion
of the first, see Frank Tannenbaum, *Slave and Citizen: The Negro in the Americas* (New York, 1946);
Stanley Elkins, *Slavery: A Problem in American Institutional and Intellectual Life* (Chicago, 1959); Herbert S.
Klein, *Slavery in the Americas: A Comparative Study of Cuba and Virginia* (Chicago, 1967); Eugene D.
Genovese, *The World the Slaveholders Made: Two Essays in Interpretation* (New York, 1969). For an exception
to this tendency, see Blackburn, *Overthrow of Colonial Slavery.*

21. But see Blackburn, *Overthrow of Colonial Slavery,* 111–
30; Sylvia R. Frey, *Water from the Rock: Black Resistance in a Revolutionary Age* (Princeton, 1991); David
Brion Davis, "American Slavery and the American
Revolution," in *Slavery and Freedom in the Age of the
American Revolution,* ed. Ira Berlin and Ronald
Hoffman (Charlottesville, Va., 1983), 262–80; Davis,
Problem of Slavery in the Age of Revolution.

22. Eugene D. Genovese, *From Rebellion to Revolution:
Afro-American Slave Revolts in the Making of the Modern World* (Baton Rouge, 1979), 82–125; Douglas R.
Egerton, *Gabriel's Rebellion: The Virginia Slave Conspiracies of 1800 and 1802* (Chapel Hill, 1993), 45–48, 160–
72; Julius Scott, "The Common Wind: Currents of
Afro-American Communication in the Age of the
Haitian Revolution" (Ph.D. diss., Duke University,
1986); Laurent Dubois, "The Haitian Revolution

and the Sale of Louisiana," *Southern Quarterly* 44 (Spring 2007): 18–41; Adam Rothman, *Slave Country: American Expansion and the Origins of the Deep South* (Cambridge, Mass., 2005); Gordon S. Brown, *Toussaint's Clause: The Founding Fathers and the Haitian Revolution* (Jackson, Miss., 2005); Alfred N. Hunt, *Haiti's Influence on Antebellum America: Slumbering Volcano in the Caribbean* (Baton Rouge, 1988). I have discussed some of these connections in "Rebel Rebel," *New Republic,* September 10, 2007, 41–47.

23. Joel H. Silbey, *Storm over Texas: The Annexation Controversy and the Road to the Civil War* (New York, 2005); Frederick Merk, *Slavery and the Annexation of Texas* (New York, 1972); Michael Craton, *Testing the Chains: Resistance to Slavery in the British West Indies* (Ithaca, 1982), 241–322; Emilia Viotti da Costa, *Crowns of Glory, Tears of Blood: The Demerara Slave Rebellion of 1823* (New York, 1994); Thomas C. Holt, *The Problem of Freedom: Race, Labor, and Politics in Jamaica and Britain, 1832–1938* (Baltimore, 1992), 3–53; William J. Cooper Jr., *Liberty and Slavery: Southern Politics to 1860* (New York, 1983), 207–12.

24. Holt, *The Problem of Freedom,* 115–309; Joe B. Wilkins, "Window on Freedom: The South's Response to the Emancipation of Slaves in the British West Indies" (Ph.D. diss., University of South Carolina, 1977). For some interesting thoughts on the relation of British emancipation and American politics,

see David Brion Davis, *Challenging the Boundaries of Slavery* (Cambridge, Mass., 2003), 61–91.

25. See, for example, Horton and Horton, *In Hope of Liberty;* James Oliver Horton, *Free People of Color: Inside the African-American Community* (Washington, D.C., 1993); Patrick Rael, *Black Identity and Black Protest in the Antebellum North* (Chapel Hill, 2002); Jane Pease and William Pease, *They Who Would Be Free: Blacks' Search for Freedom, 1831–1860* (New York, 1974); Nash, *Forging Freedom;* White, *Somewhat More Independent;* Harris, *In the Shadow of Slavery;* Eddie S. Glaude Jr., *Exodus! Religion, Race, and Nation in Early Nineteenth-Century Black America* (Chicago, 2000); Richard S. Newman, *The Transformation of American Abolitionism: Fighting Slavery in the Early Republic* (Chapel Hill, 2002).

26. See Eugene D. Genovese, *Roll, Jordan, Roll: The World the Slaves Made* (New York, 1974); John Blassingame, *The Slave Community: Plantation Life in the Antebellum South* (New York, 1972); Herbert G. Gutman, *The Black Family in Slavery and Freedom, 1750–1925* (New York, 1976); Roger D. Abrahams, *Singing the Master: The Emergence of African-American Culture in the Plantation South* (New York, 1992); Charles Joyner, *Down by the Riverside: A South Carolina Slave Community* (Urbana, Ill., 1984); Thomas L. Webber, *Deep Like the Rivers: Education in the Slave Quarter Community, 1831–1865* (New York, 1978); Albert J. Raboteau, *Slave Reli-*

gion: The "Invisible Institution" in the Antebellum South (New York, 1978).

27. On the encounters of the Civil War and Reconstruction years, see Ira Berlin et al., eds., *Freedom: A Documentary History of Emancipation, 1861-1867,* ser. 1 and 2, 4 vols. (Cambridge, U.K., 1982-1993); Leon Litwack, *Been in the Storm So Long: The Aftermath of Slavery* (New York, 1979); Willie Lee Rose, *Rehearsal for Reconstruction: The Port Royal Experiment* (Indianapolis, 1964); Foner, *Reconstruction.* For one effort to link northern and southern communities of African descent, see Horton, *Free People of Color,* 55-71.

28. I briefly raised this conceptual possibility in *A Nation under Our Feet: Black Political Struggles in the Rural South from Slavery to the Great Migration* (Cambridge, Mass., 2003), 57. But also I discovered that Ira Berlin and Thomas P. Slaughter have been thinking along similar lines. See Berlin, *Generations of Captivity: A History of African-American Slaves* (Cambridge, Mass., 2003), 233-37; Slaughter, *Bloody Dawn: The Christiana Riot and Racial Violence in the Antebellum North* (New York, 1991), 49.

29. There is a very large literature on marronage in various parts of the Americas, but for some important studies see Richard Price, ed., *Maroon Societies: Rebel Slave Communities in the Americas,* 2nd ed. (Baltimore, 1979); Craton, *Testing the Chains,* 61-96; Stuart Schwartz, *Slaves, Peasants, and Rebels: Reconsidering*

Brazilian Slavery (Urbana, Ill., 1992), 103–36; David P. Geggus, *Haitian Revolutionary Studies* (Bloomington, Ind., 2002), 69–80; Jean Fouchard, *The Haitian Maroons: Liberty or Death* (New York, 1981); Genovese, *Rebellion to Revolution,* 51–81.

30. See Jane Landers, *Black Society in Spanish Florida* (Urbana, Ill., 1999), 29–60; Landers, "Slave Resistance on the Southeastern Frontier," in *Look Away: The U.S. South in New World Studies,* ed. Jon Smith and Deborah Cohn (Durham, N.C., 2004); Peter H. Wood, *Black Majority: Negroes in Colonial South Carolina from 1670 to the Stono Rebellion* (New York, 1974); Gerald Mullin, *Flight and Rebellion: Slave Resistance in Eighteenth-Century Virginia* (New York, 1972), 34–82; Kenneth Wiggins Porter, *The Negro on the American Frontier* (New York, 1971); James H. Merrell, *The Indians' New World: Catawbas and Their Neighbors from European Contact through the Era of Removal* (New York, 1991); Berlin, *Many Thousands Gone,* 87–88, 120–22, 169–70, 305–6, 328–29, 339–40; Gwendolyn Midlo Hall, *Africans in Colonial Louisiana: The Development of Afro-Creole Culture in the Eighteenth Century* (Baton Rouge, 1992), 113–18, 201–36; Daniel H. Usner, *Indians, Settlers, and Slaves in a Frontier Exchange Economy: The Lower Mississippi Valley before 1783* (Chapel Hill, 1992).

31. Herbert Aptheker, "Maroons within the Present Limits of the United States," *Journal of Negro History*

24 (April 1939): 167–84; John Hope Franklin and Loren Schweninger, *Runaway Slaves: Rebels on the Plantation* (New York, 1999), 86–89; Porter, *Negro on American Frontier,* 210–59; Hugo Prosper Leaming, *Hidden Americans: Maroons of Virginia and the Carolinas* (New York, 1995).

32. On these Brazilian and Caribbean maroons, see R. K. Kent, "Palmares: An African State in Brazil," Roger Bastide, "The Other Quilombos," Stuart B. Schwartz, "The Mocambo: Slave Resistance in Colonial Bahia," and Orlando Patterson, "Slavery and Slave Revolts: A Sociohistorical Analysis of the First Maroon War, 1665–1740," all in Price, ed. *Maroon Societies,* 170–226, 246–92; John Gabriel Stedman, *Narrative of a Five-Year Expedition against the Revolted Negroes of Surinam,* ed. Richard Price and Sally Price (1790; rept., Baltimore, 1988); Craton, *Testing the Chains,* 61–96; Alvin O. Thompson, *Flight to Freedom: African Runaways and Maroons in the Americas* (Kingston, Jamaica, 2006); Genovese, *Rebellion to Revolution,* 51–81.

33. See Hilary Beckles, "From Land to Sea: Runaway Barbados Slaves and Servants, 1630–1700," *Slavery and Abolition* 6 (December 1985): 79–94; N. A. T. Hall, "Maritime Maroons: *Grand Marronage* from the Danish West Indies," in *Caribbean Slavery in the Atlantic World,* ed. Verene Shepherd and Hilary McD. Beckles (Kingston, Jamaica, 2000), 905–18;

Anthony McFarlane, "Cimarrones and Palenques: Runaways and Resistance in Colonial Colombia," *Slavery and Abolition* 6 (December 1985): 131-51; Schwartz, *Slaves, Peasants, and Rebels,* 103-36; João José Reis, *Slave Rebellion in Brazil: The Muslim Uprising of 1835 in Bahia,* trans. Arthur Brakel (Baltimore, 1993), 40-69, 153; Carolyn E. Fick, *The Making of Haiti: The Saint Domingue Revolution from Below* (Knoxville, Tenn., 1990); Craton, *Testing the Chains,* 211-38; David Barry Gaspar, *Bondmen and Rebels: A Study of Master-Slave Relations in Antigua* (Baltimore, 1985), 171-84; Flavio dos Santos, "A 'Safe Haven': Runaway Slaves, Mocambos, and Borders in Colonial Amazonia, Brazil," *Hispanic American Historical Review* 82 (August 2002): 469-98; Patrick J. Carroll, "Mandinga: The Evolution of a Mexican Runaway Slave Community, 1735-1827," *Comparative Studies in Society and History* 19 (April 1977): 488-505. It is important to distinguish, as specialists do, between what is known as *grand marronage,* by which is meant flight with the intention to construct or join communities of runaways, and *petit marronage,* usually individual flight in response to a particular abuse.

34. For the population figures, see Leonard P. Curry, *The Free Black in Urban America, 1800–1850* (Chicago, 1986), 249; Joe William Trotter Jr., *River Jordan: African-American Urban Life in the Ohio Valley*

(Lexington, Ky., 1998), 26–29; Michael Mangin, "Freemen in Theory: Race, Society, and Politics in Ross County, Ohio, 1796–1850" (Ph.D. diss., University of California, San Diego, 2002); Rael, *Black Identity and Black Protest,* 39–40.

35. See Harris, *In the Shadow of Slavery,* 72–77; White, *Somewhat More Independent,* 171–79; Nash, *Forging Freedom,* 158–71, 248–50; Henry Louis Taylor Jr. and Vicky Dula, "The Black Residential Experience and Community Formation in Antebellum Cincinnati," in *Race and the City: Work, Community, and Protest in Cincinnati, 1820–1870,* ed. Henry Louis Taylor Jr. (Urbana, Ill., 1993), 96–125; Xenia E. Cord, "Black Rural Settlements in Indiana before 1860," in *Indiana's African-American Heritage: Essays from Black History News and Notes,* ed. Wilma L. Gibbs (Indianapolis, 1993), 99–110.

36. The process of migration or, in this case, marronage, is not very well studied, but for some important evidence and ideas, see Horton, "Links to Bondage: Free Blacks and the Underground Railroad," in *Free People of Color,* 53–74; Slaughter, *Bloody Dawn,* 39–49; Fergus M. Bordewich, *Bound for Canaan: The Underground Railroad and the War for the Soul of America* (New York, 2005).

37. Horton and Horton, *In Hope of Liberty,* 101–54; Cord, "Black Rural Settlements in Indiana," 99–102; Henry L. Taylor, "On Slavery's Fringe: City-Building

and Black Community Development in Cincinnati, 1800–1850," *Ohio History* 95 (Winter/Spring 1986): 5–33; Rael, *Black Identity and Black Protest,* 12–53; Harris, *In the Shadow of Slavery,* 121–33; Nash, *Forging Freedom,* 172–279; David Waldstreicher, *In the Midst of Perpetual Fetes: The Making of American Nationalism, 1776–1820* (Chapel Hill, 1997), 294–348; Newman, *The Transformation of American Abolitionism;* Glaude, *Exodus!* 84–95.

38. David Ruggles et al., "First Annual Report of the Committee of Vigilance for the Protection of People of Color" (1837), in *Pamphlets of Protest: An Anthology of Early African-American Protest Literature, 1790–1860,* ed. Richard Newman, Patrick Rael, and Philip Lapsansky (New York, 2001), 150; Martin Delany, *Blake; or, The Huts of America* (1859–62; rept., Boston, 1970), 61.

39. Carol Wilson, "Active Vigilance Is the Price of Liberty: Black Self-Defense against Fugitive Slave Recapture and Kidnapping of Free Blacks," in *Antislavery Violence: Sectional, Racial, and Cultural Conflict in Antebellum America,* ed. John R. McKivigan and Stanley Harrold (Knoxville, Tenn., 1999), 108; William Parker, "The Freedman's Story" (1866), in *I Was Born a Slave: An Anthology of Classic Slave Narratives,* ed. Yuval Taylor, 2 vols. (Chicago, 1999), 2:755, 769.

40. "First Annual Report of the Committee of Vigi-

lance," 149–50; Wilson, "Active Vigilance Is the Price of Liberty," 108–19; Douglass, *My Bondage and My Freedom,* 207–8.

41. For the best and most powerful treatment of the Christiana riot, see Slaughter, *Bloody Dawn.* Also see Parker, "Freedmen's Story," 764–86; Ella Forbes, "'By My Own Right Arm': Redemptive Violence and the 1851 Christiana, Pennsylvania Resistance," *Journal of Negro History* 83 (June 1998): 159–66.

42. Slaughter, *Bloody Dawn,* 44–47; Leonard Richards, *"Gentlemen of Property and Standing": Anti-Abolitionist Mobs in Jacksonian America* (New York, 1970); Harris, *In the Shadow of Slavery,* 194–98, 220, 227, 247–48; Horton and Horton, *In Hope of Liberty,* 243–44; Darrel E. Bigham, *On Jordan's Banks: Emancipation and Its Aftermath in the Ohio River Valley* (Lexington, Ky., 2006), 40–42.

43. On fugitive slaves moving from place to place, unsuccessfully searching for safe haven in the territorial United States, see Roper, *Narrative of the Adventures and Escape,* 76–84; Smallwood, *Narrative of Thomas Smallwood,* 44–46; Brown and Stearns, *Narrative of Henry Box Brown,* 65; Brown, *Narrative of William Wells Brown,* 105, 110; Henson, *Life of Josiah Henson,* 48; "William and Ellen Craft Interview" (1851), in *Slave Testimony: Two Centuries of Letters, Speeches, Interviews, and Autobiographies,* ed. John W. Blassingame (Baton Rouge, 1977), 268–74. On the

black codes of the lower Midwest, see Berwanger, *Frontier against Slavery,* 30–59.

44. Campbell, *Slave Catchers,* 87–88, 112–16; Slaughter, *Bloody Dawn,* 94–138; Newman, *Transformation of American Abolitionism,* 107–51; Horton and Horton, *In Hope of Liberty,* 203–68; Morris, *Free Men All,* passim, esp. 42–58, 107–29, 130–85. As Stanley Campbell points out, even as states in the Northeast and Midwest passed personal liberty laws, the majority of northerners still favored the enforcement of the Fugitive Slave Law, and the enforcement of the Fugitive Slave Law proved to be highly effective.

45. For important studies of black political activity and thought in this period that focus chiefly on the leadership, see Rael, *Black Identity and Black Protest;* Newman et al., *Pamphlets of Protest,* 1–31 and passim; Glaude, *Exodus!;* Pease and Pease, *They Who Would Be Free;* Horton and Horton, *In Hope of Liberty;* John Stauffer, *Black Hearts of Men: Radical Abolitionists and the Transformation of Race* (Cambridge, Mass., 2002). For a more grassroots perspective, see Harris, *In the Shadow of Slavery;* Newman, *Transformation of American Abolitionism;* Howard H. Bell, "Expressions of Negro Militancy in the North, 1840–1860," *Journal of Negro History* 45 (January 1960): 11–20.

46. David Walker, *Appeal to the Coloured Citizens of the World,* ed. Peter P. Hinks (1829; rept., University Park, Pa., 2000). The best, and most recent, study of

Walker's life and thought is Peter P. Hinks's impressive *To Awaken My Afflicted Brethren: David Walker and the Problem of Antebellum Slave Resistance* (University Park, Pa., 1997).

47. Delany's novel appeared in the *Anglo-African Magazine* between January and July 1859 and in the *Weekly Anglo-African* between November 1861 and February 1862. It was not published in book form until the 1970 edition.

48. William Webb, *The History of William Webb, Composed by Himself* (Detroit, 1873), 14, 23, 26.

49. Ibid., 13–30. On the acquisition and circulation of political knowledge and information, see Douglass, *My Bondage and My Freedom,* 103–4, 106–7; Charles Ball, *Fifty Years in Chains; or, The Life of An American Slave* (New York, 1859), 19–20; "Narrative of James Curry," in Blassingame, *Slave Testimony,* 135; Scott, "Common Wind," 272–74; Solomon Northup, *Twelve Years a Slave: Narrative of Solomon Northup, a Citizen of New-York* (Auburn, N.Y., 1853), 188–90; Merton Dillon, *Slavery Attacked: Southern Slaves and Their Allies, 1619–1865* (Baton Rouge, 1990), 76, 139–41. For an important treatment of slave communication in one locality, see Anthony E. Kaye, *Joining Places: Slave Neighborhoods in the Old South* (Chapel Hill, 2007).

50. It should be noted that even Lincoln's thinking on the emancipation process, in evidence through the

Preliminary Emancipation Proclamation of September 1862, envisioned a gradual emancipation unfolding over a period of, perhaps, thirty-five years. See Ira Berlin et al., *Slaves No More: Three Essays on Emancipation* (New York, 1992), 29–30. On gradualism in the abolition of slavery and other forms of servile labor, see Zilversmit, *First Emancipation;* Green, *British Slave Emancipation;* Eric Foner, *Nothing but Freedom: Emancipation and Its Legacy* (Baton Rouge, 1982), 8–30; Arthur L. Stinchcombe, *Sugar Island Slavery in the Age of Enlightenment: The Political Economy of the Caribbean World* (Princeton, 1995), 175–318; Blum, *The End of the Old Order in Rural Europe,* 357–441.

51. On sectionalism as a deep and enduring force in American politics, see Richard Franklin Bensel, *Sectionalism and American Political Development, 1880–1980* (Madison, Wisc., 1984). On the antebellum critique of the slave South, see Eric Foner, *Free Soil, Free Labor, Free Men: The Ideology of the Republican Party before the Civil War* (New York, 1970). On the relationship between sectionalism, regionalism, and federal state building in the late nineteenth and early twentieth centuries, see Natalie J. Ring, *The Paradox of the New South: The Problem of Region and Race* (Athens, Ga., forthcoming).

52. The comparative history of emancipations and reconstructions, after all, draws us to the transition

from slavery to freedom and to the varied efforts to "reconstruct" the social and political relations of postemancipation societies. See, for example, Foner, *Nothing but Freedom;* C. Vann Woodward, "Emancipations and Reconstructions: A Comparative Study," in his *The Future of the Past* (New York, 1989), 145–66; Peter Kolchin, "Some Thoughts on Emancipation in Comparative Perspective: Russia and the United States," *Slavery and Abolition* 11 (December 1990): 351–67.

2. Did We Miss the Greatest Slave Rebellion in Modern History?

1. R. Q. Millard et al. to Brig. Gen. Mercer [August 1862], and James A. Seddon to Gen. G. T. Beauregard, November 30, 1862, both in *Freedom: A Documentary History of Emancipation, 1861–1867, The Black Military Experience,* ed. Ira Berlin et al., ser. 2 (New York, 1982), 571–72.

2. Rev. C. C. Jones to Lt. Charles C. Jones Jr., July 21, 1862, in *The Children of Pride: A True Story of Georgia and the Civil War,* ed. Robert Manson Myers (New Haven, 1972), 935; Kate Stone, *Brokenburn: The Journal of Kate Stone, 1861–1868,* ed. John Q. Anderson (Baton Rouge, 1955), 28; Alexander F. Pugh Plantation Diary, entry for July 3, 1863, Alexander F. Pugh Family Papers, Louisiana State University Archives, Baton Rouge; Anonymous to Friend, January 3,

1863, Department of the Gulf, Record Group 393, Part 1, Letters Received, ser. 1756, National Archives, Washington, D.C. (C-521); C. Peter Ripley, *Slaves and Freedmen in Civil War Louisiana* (Baton Rouge, 1976), 97; Bell I. Wiley, *Southern Negroes, 1861–1865* (New Haven, 1938), 74-75.

3. Herbert Aptheker, *American Negro Slave Revolts* (1943; rept., New York, 1993), 363-67. W. E. B. Du Bois described the flight of the slaves from their plantations and farms during the Civil War as a "general strike," which effectively deprived their owners and the Confederacy of slave labor and support and offered it to the Union. He also used the term *mutiny,* but he was careful to write that the "Negroes showed no disposition to strike the one terrible blow which brought black men to freedom in Haiti and which in all history has been used by all slaves and justified . . . insurrection." See Du Bois, *Black Reconstruction in America: An Essay toward a History of the Part Which Black Folk Played in the Attempt to Reconstruct Democracy in America, 1860–1880* (New York, 1935), 55-83. Among present-day historians, only Merton L. Dillon has argued that "the war assumed the character of a slave uprising." See his *Slavery Attacked: Southern Slaves and Their Allies, 1619–1865* (Baton Rouge, 1990), 243-66.

4. On the Confederacy see Ira Berlin et al., eds., *Freedom: A Documentary History of Emancipation, 1861–*

1867, The Destruction of Slavery ser. 1 (New York, 1985), 1:663–818; Armstead L. Robinson, *Bitter Fruits of Bondage: The Demise of Slavery and the Collapse of the Confederacy, 1861–1865* (Charlottesville, Va., 2005), 37–57; Steven Hahn, *The Roots of Southern Populism: Yeoman Farmers and the Transformation of the Georgia Upcountry, 1850–1890* (New York, 1983), 116–33. On the Union see Gen. B. F. Butler to Gov. Thomas H. Hicks, April 23, 1861, Major-Gen. George B. McClellan to Col. Irvine, May 26, 1861, Major-Gen. McClellan to Col. J. B. Steedman, May 26, 1861, F. J. Porter to U.S. Troops of This Department, June 3, 1861, all in *The War of the Rebellion: A Compilation of the Official Records of the Union and Confederate Armies*, 130 vols. (Washington, D.C., 1880–1901), ser. 1, 2:593, 47–48, 661–62; James M. McPherson, *The Struggle for Equality: Abolitionists and the Negro in the Civil War and Reconstruction* (Princeton, 1964), 55–59; William K. Klingaman, *Abraham Lincoln and the Road to Emancipation, 1861–1865* (New York, 2001), 58–59; Benjamin Quarles, *The Negro in the Civil War* (Boston, 1953), 65.

5. McClellan to Irvine, May 26, 1861, in *War of the Rebellion,* ser. 1, 2:47.

6. Berlin et al., *Freedom,* ser. 1, 1:22–27, 61, 103–7, 187–89, 249–56; Robinson, *Bitter Fruits of Bondage,* 138–45; Joel Williamson, *After Slavery: The Negro in South Carolina during Reconstruction, 1861–1877* (Chapel Hill, 1965), 4–5; John Eaton, *Grant, Lincoln, and the Freed-*

men: Reminiscences of the Civil War (1907; rept., New York, 1969), 1–2.

7. The best estimates on the number of slaves who had reached Union lines by this point are to be found in Ira Berlin et al., eds., *Freedom: A Documentary History of Emancipation. The Wartime Genesis of Free Labor: The Lower South,* ser. 1 (New York, 1990), 3:77–80.

8. Louis Gerteis, *From Contraband to Freedman: Federal Policy toward Southern Blacks, 1861–1865* (Westport, Conn., 1973), 11–14; Berlin et al., *Freedom,* ser. 1, 1:59–61, 72; Robert F. Engs, *Freedom's First Generation: Black Hampton, Virginia, 1861–1890* (Philadelphia, 1979), 25–28; Edward McPherson, *The Political History of the United States of America during the Great Rebellion* (New York, 1864), 195–97, 237–38.

9. J. Carlyle Sitterson, *Sugar Country: The Cane Sugar Industry in the South, 1753–1950* (Lexington, Ky., 1953), 209–10; Wiley, *Southern Negroes,* 74–75; Ripley, *Slaves and Freedmen,* 22–23; George H. Hepworth, *The Whip, the Hoe, and the Sword: The Gulf Department in '63* (Boston, 1864), 29–30; Berlin et al., *Freedom,* ser. 1, 2:37, 445, 636; 3:479–80, 785.

10. McPherson, *Struggle for Equality,* 192–93; Quarles, *Negro in the Civil War,* 22–35; William Cheek and Aimee Lee Cheek, *John Mercer Langston and the Fight for Black Freedom, 1829–65* (Urbana, Ill., 1989), 383–87.

11. *Christian Recorder,* January 18, 1862; Joseph T. Wilson, *The Black Phalanx: A History of Negro Soldiers of the United States in the Wars of 1775–1812, 1861–1865* (Hartford, 1890), 187–88; Berlin et al., *Freedom,* 37–73.

12. We can only estimate the proportion of black soldiers in the Union Army by the last year of the war, and the estimate itself is somewhat contingent. In January 1865, 959,460 soldiers were enrolled in the Union Army, of whom 123,156 were black (12.8 percent), but of the total only 620,924 soldiers were "present," which pushes the black proportion to as much as 19.8 percent. See Thomas L. Livermore, *Numbers and Losses in the Civil War in America, 1861–1865* (Bloomington, Ind., 1957), 47; E. B. Long with Barbara Long, *The Civil War Day by Day: An Almanac, 1861–1865* (New York, 1971), 706; Berlin et al., *Freedom,* ser. 2, 733.

13. Jefferson Davis to Govs. Shorter, Rector, Milton, Brown, Hawes, Moore, Pettus, Jackson, Vance, Pickens, Harris, Lubbock, and Letcher, November 26, 1862, in *The Papers of Jefferson Davis,* ed. Lynda Lasswell Crist et al., 11 vols. (Baton Rouge, 1971–2003), 8:516; General Orders No. 111, December 24, 1862, in *War of the Rebellion,* ser. 2, 5:795–97; Berlin et al., *Freedom,* ser. 2, 567–68; Dudley Taylor Cornish, *The Sable Arm: Negro Troops in the Union Army, 1861–*

1865 (1956; rept., New York, 1966), 160–62; John W. Graham to William A. Graham, March 13, 1864, in *The Papers of William Alexander Graham,* ed. Max R. Williams, 8 vols. (Raleigh, N.C., 1957–92), 6:42–43; Drew Gilpin Faust, *This Republic of Suffering: Death and the American Civil War* (New York, 2008), 53. Davis's order also called for executing "all commissioned officers of the United States when found serving in company with armed slaves in insurrection against the authorities of the different states of this Confederacy." In May 1863 the Confederate Congress ratified Davis's order.

14. On the War Department's orders, see Cornish, *Sable Arm,* 160–80.

15. On the sacking of estates, see Meta Morris Grimball Diary, entry for August 4, 1863, Southern Historical Collection, Chapel Hill, N.C.; Willie Lee Rose, *Rehearsal for Reconstruction: The Port Royal Experiment* (Indianapolis, 1964), 106–7; Leslie A. Schwalm, *A Hard Fight for We: Women's Transition from Slavery to Freedom in South Carolina* (Urbana, Ill., 1997), 93–94. I am grateful to Stephanie McCurry, who is completing an in-depth analysis in her book, *Confederate Crucible: The Unfranchised and the Political Transformation of the Civil War South* (Cambridge, Mass., forthcoming), for bringing this material to my attention.

16. For one of the best treatments of such a conspiracy,

see Winthrop D. Jordan, *Tumult and Silence at Second Creek: An Inquiry into a Civil War Slave Conspiracy* (Baton Rouge, 1993). Also see Robinson, *Bitter Fruits of Bondage,* 42–45; Aptheker, *American Negro Slave Revolts,* 359–67; Dillon, *Slavery Attacked,* 260–62; Wiley, *Southern Negroes,* 67–68, 81–83.

17. For excellent treatments of slave rebellions, or conspiracies, in the Americas that help us see the range of goals and practices, see Michael Craton, *Testing the Chains: Resistance to Slavery in the British West Indies* (Ithaca, 1982); Laurent Dubois, *Avengers of the New World: The Story of the Haitian Revolution* (Cambridge, Mass., 2004); Laurent Dubois, *A Colony of Citizens: Revolution and Slave Emancipation in the French Caribbean, 1787–1804* (Chapel Hill, 2004); David Geggus, *Haitian Revolutionary Studies* (Bloomington, Ind., 2002); Emilia Viotti da Costa, *Crowns of Glory, Tears of Blood: The Demerara Slave Rebellion of 1823* (New York, 1994); João José Reis, *Slave Rebellion in Brazil: The Muslim Uprising of 1835 in Bahia,* trans. Arthur Brakel (Baltimore, 1993); Mark M. Smith, ed., *Stono: Documenting and Interpreting a Southern Slave Revolt* (Columbia, S.C., 2005); Robert L. Paquette, *Sugar Is Made with Blood: The Conspiracy of La Escalera and the Conflict between Empires over Slavery in Cuba* (Middletown, Conn., 1988); Douglas R. Egerton, *Gabriel's Rebellion: The Virginia Slave Conspiracies of 1800 and 1802* (Chapel Hill, 1993); Eugene

D. Genovese, *From Rebellion to Revolution: Afro-American Slave Revolts in the Making of the Modern World* (Baton Rouge, 1979).

18. Genovese, *From Rebellion to Revolution,* 128–29; Dillon, *Slavery Attacked,* 135, 156, 187–88; Wendell Addington, "Slave Insurrections in Texas," *Journal of Negro History* 35 (October 1950): 413; Harvey Wish, "American Slave Insurrections before 1861," *Journal of Negro History* 22 (July 1937): 299–300; Aptheker, *American Negro Slave Revolts,* 265, 277, 284–85, 328–29, 345–46; Michael P. Johnson, "Denmark Vesey and His Co-Conspirators," *William and Mary Quarterly* 58 (October 2001): 960–71.

19. Booker T. Washington, *Up from Slavery,* ed. William L. Andrews (1901; rept., New York, 1996), 10; Charles L. Perdue et al., eds., *Weevils in the Wheat: Interviews with Virginia Ex-Slaves* (Bloomington, Ind., 1976), 216; Stone, *Brokenburn,* 28, 33; Robinson, *Bitter Fruits of Bondage,* 37–45; Clarence L. Mohr, *On the Threshold of Freedom: Masters and Slaves in Civil War Georgia* (Athens, Ga., 1986), 36–37; Randolph B. Campbell, *An Empire for Slavery: The Peculiar Institution in Texas, 1821–1865* (Baton Rouge, 1989), 224–28; Dillon, *Slavery Attacked,* 240–42; John K. Betterworth, *Confederate Mississippi: The People and the Policies of a Cotton State in Wartime* (Baton Rouge, 1943), 162.

20. John Blassingame, ed., *Slave Testimony: Two Centuries*

of Letters, Speeches, Interviews, and Autobiographies (Baton Rouge, 1977), 607–8 (emphasis in original). I have discussed slave communication at length in *A Nation under Our Feet: Black Political Struggles in the Rural South from Slavery to the Great Migration* (Cambridge, Mass., 2003), especially chaps. 1, 2, and 3. But also see the new work of Susan E. O'Donovan, "Trunk Lines, Land Lines, and Local Exchanges: Operationalizing the Grapevine Telegraph" (paper presented at the Gilder Lehrman Center, Yale University, December 2006).

21. Admiral David Dixon Porter, *Incidents and Anecdotes of the Civil War* (New York, 1886), 89–91. For particularly powerful evidence of communication between contrabands and "the black men still in slavery," see the testimony of C. B. Wilder, the Superintendent of Contrabands at Fortress Monroe, before the American Freedmen's Inquiry Commission in May 1863, in Berlin et al., *Freedom,* ser. 1, 1:88–90.

22. Quarles, *Negro in the Civil War,* 109–10; Mohr, *On the Threshold of Freedom,* 84–85; Wilson, *Black Phalanx,* 130–31; Joseph T. Glatthaar, *Forged in Battle: The Civil War Alliance of Black Soldiers and White Officers* (New York, 1990), 72–75; Edwin S. Redkey, *A Grand Army of Black Men: Letters from African-American Soldiers in the Union Army, 1861–1865* (Cambridge, U.K., 1992), 84–85; Berlin et al., *Freedom,* ser. 2, 13, 55–56, 116–22;

"Abstract of a visit of Major Yarrington to plantations of Dr. Knapp, Ducross et al.," September 3, 1863, in Berlin et al., *Freedom,* ser. 1, 3:461.

23. See, for example, Berlin et al., *Freedom,* ser. 2, 362–405; James M. McPherson, *The Negro's Civil War: How American Negroes Felt and Acted during the War for the Union* (New York, 1965), 193–204; Glatthaar, *Forged in Battle,* 169–76; Leon F. Litwack, *Been in the Storm So Long: The Aftermath of Slavery* (New York, 1979), 79–87; Cornish, *Sable Arm,* 160–80; *New Orleans Tribune,* November 15, 1864, December 29, 1864, January 15, 1865; Eric Foner, *Reconstruction: America's Unfinished Revolution, 1863–1877* (New York, 1988), 35–76.

24. On the conflicts provoked by rumors of land reform in the latter part of 1865, see Steven Hahn, "'Extravagant Expectations' of Freedom: Rumour, Political Struggle, and the Christmas Insurrection Scare of 1865 in the American South," *Past and Present* 157, no. 1 (November 1997): 122–58; Steven Hahn et al., eds., *Freedom: A Documentary History of Emancipation, 1861–1867, Land and Labor in 1865,* ser. 3 (Chapel Hill, 2008), 1: 796–908.

25. Gary B. Nash, *The Forgotten Fifth: African Americans in the Age of Revolution* (Cambridge, Mass., 2006), 30–31 and passim. For studies of these rebellions, see Smith, *Stono;* Craton, *Testing the Chains;* Stuart Schwartz, *Slaves, Peasants, and Rebels: Reconsidering*

Brazilian Slavery (Urbana, Ill., 1992), 103–36; Egerton, *Gabriel's Rebellion;* Adam Rothman, *Slave Country: American Expansion and the Origins of the Deep South* (Cambridge, Mass., 2005), 109–17; Viotti da Costa, *Crowns of Glory, Tears of Blood.*

26. For recent, and influential, treatments of the rebellion in Saint Domingue, see Dubois, *Avengers of the New World;* Madison Smartt Bell, *Toussaint Louverture: A Biography* (New York, 2007); Geggus, *Haitian Revolutionary Studies;* Carolyn Fick, *The Making of Haiti: The Saint Domingue Revolution from Below* (Knoxville, Tenn., 1990); Laurent Dubois and John D. Garrigus, eds., *Slave Revolution in the Caribbean, 1789–1804: A Brief History with Documents* (Boston, 2006). Also see the still powerful C. L. R. James, *The Black Jacobins: Toussaint L'Ouverture and the San Domingo Revolution* (New York, 1938).

27. Geggus, *Haitian Revolutionary Studies,* 12.

28. Bell, *Toussaint Louverture,* 28. Bell's is chiefly a figurative allusion, and, in fact, the historian John K. Thornton has made a powerful argument that west-central African, and particularly Kongolese, military traditions and former soldiers made decisive contributions to the success of Saint Domingue's slave armies, especially in the northern province. As Thornton points out, a majority of the slaves in Saint Domingue, particularly those who

would fight steadily during the revolution, had been born in Africa (probably on either the Lower Guinea or Angola coast) and had served in African armies before their enslavement. See Thornton, "African Soldiers in the Haitian Revolution," *Journal of Caribbean History* 25 (1992): 58–81.

29. Clearly, the new nation that emerged as a result of the Haitian Revolution was radically different from the newly constituted nation that emerged in the United States as a result of the Civil War and slave rebellion. In Haiti former slaves and *gens de couleur* became rulers and, in bloody struggles and increasingly desperate circumstances, attempted to make national policy. In the United States, former slaves and free people of color were, by and large, the allies and clients of white Republican rulers nationally, although they would wield much more power and leverage on the state and local levels in the former Confederate South until the white Republicans abandoned them. Again, my point here is not that the rebellions in Saint Domingue and in the Civil War South were the same or had identical outcomes; far from it. My point is rather that they had dynamics in common and that those dynamics should encourage us to think of what the slaves did in the United States as a rebellion.

30. For these examples I am indebted to Matthew J. Clavin's interesting "American Toussaints: Symbol,

Subversion, and the Black Atlantic Tradition in the American Civil War," *Slavery and Abolition* 28 (April 2007): 87–113.

31. Frederick Douglass, "Men of Color, to Arms!" in *The Life and Writings of Frederick Douglass,* ed. Philip S. Foner, 5 vols. (New York, 1952), 3:319; *New Orleans Tribune,* October 6, 1864, November 15, 1864, January 15, 1865; *Christian Recorder,* January 16, 1864; Clavin, "American Toussaints," 96–97; Lt. Edward M. Stoeber to Brev. Maj. S. M. Taylor, July 24, 1865, Bureau of Refugees, Freedmen, and Abandoned Lands, Record Group 105, S-5 1865, Registered Letters Received, ser. 2922, Records of the South Carolina Assistant Commissioner, National Archives, Washington, D.C. (emphasis in original). Stoeber was a first lieutenant in the 104th U.S.C.T., and Delany, one of the few African Americans who gained a commissioned rank, was a major.

32. On the importance and triumph of the "reconciliationist" narrative, see David W. Blight, *Race and Reunion: The Civil War in American Memory* (Cambridge, Mass., 2001). On the "brothers' war," see Stephanie McCurry, " 'The Brothers' War'?: Women, Slaves, and Popular Politics in the Civil War South" (paper presented at the meeting of the Southern Association of Women's Historians, Fort Worth, Tex., November 1999).

33. George Cary Eggleston, *A Rebel's Recollections* (Cam-

bridge, Mass., 1875); Alice Fahs, *The Imagined Civil War: Popular Literature of the North and South, 1861–1865* (Chapel Hill, 2001), 150–94; Blight, *Race and Reunion,* 255–99; Thomas J. Pressley, *Americans Interpret Their Civil War* (New York, 1965), 81–126 (emphasis in original).

34. Joseph E. Roy, "Our Indebtedness to the Negroes for Their Conduct during the War," *New Englander and Yale Review* (November 1889): 353–55; James Ford Rhodes, *History of the Civil War, 1861–1865* (New York, 1917), 380–81.

35. E. Merton Coulter, *The Confederate States of America* (Baton Rouge, 1950), 255–66. Also see Walter Lynwood Fleming, *Civil War and Reconstruction in Alabama* (1901; rept., Spartanburg, S.C., 1969), 210–11; Betterworth, *Confederate Mississippi,* 161–72.

36. George Washington Williams, *History of the Negro Troops in the War of the Rebellion, 1861–1865* (New York, 1888); Blight, *Race and Reunion,* 300–337; Kathleen Ann Clark, *Defining Moments: African American Commemoration and Political Culture in the South, 1865–1913* (Chapel Hill, 2005); William H. Wiggins Jr., *O Freedom! Afro-American Emancipation Celebrations* (Knoxville, Tenn., 1987).

37. Booker T. Washington, *The Story of the Negro,* 2 vols. (New York, 1909), 2:6; Charles H. Wesley, "The Employment of Negroes as Soldiers in the Confederate Army," *Journal of Negro History* 4 (July 1919): 240–41;

Bertram W. Doyle, "Some Observations on Progress in Race Relations Prior to and Since 1868," *Journal of Negro History* 18 (January 1933): 14; Benjamin Brawley, *Social History of the American Negro* (New York, 1921), 257; Harvey Wish, "Slave Disloyalty under the Confederacy," *Journal of Negro History* 23 (October 1938): 449. Also see William Sinclair, *The Aftermath of Slavery: A Study of the Condition and Environment of the American Negro* (1905; rept., Chicago, 1969); Carter G. Woodson, *The Negro in Our History* (Washington, D.C., 1922), 361–63.

38. Du Bois, *Black Reconstruction in America,* 55–83. On the writing of the book and the contemporary response to it, see David Levering Lewis, *W. E. B. Du Bois: The Fight for Equality and the American Century, 1919–1963* (New York, 2000), 349–87.

39. John Hope Franklin, *From Slavery to Freedom: A History of Negro Americans* (1947; rept., New York, 1969), 271–96; Quarles, *Negro in the Civil War;* Cornish, *Sable Arm;* Williams, *Negro Troops in the War of the Rebellion;* Wilson, *The Black Phalanx.*

40. See, for example, John L. Thomas, *The Liberator, William Lloyd Garrison: A Biography* (New York, 1963); Aileen Kraditor, *Means and Ends in American Abolitionism: Garrison and His Critics on Strategy and Tactics, 1834–1850* (New York, 1969); W. R. Brock, *An American Crisis: Congress and Reconstruction* (London, 1963); Lawanda Cox and John H. Cox, *Politics, Principle, and*

Prejudice, 1865–1866 (New York, 1963); Rose, *Rehearsal for Reconstruction;* McPherson, *Struggle for Equality;* Otto H. Olsen, *Carpetbagger's Crusade: The Life of Albion Winegar Tourgée* (Baltimore, 1965); Kenneth Stampp, *The Era of Reconstruction, 1865–1877* (New York, 1965); Hans L. Trefousse, *The Radical Republicans: Lincoln's Vanguard for Racial Justice* (New York, 1969).

41. Kenneth Stampp, *The Peculiar Institution: Slavery in the Antebellum South* (New York, 1956); John W. Blassingame, *The Slave Community: Plantation Life in the Antebellum South* (New York, 1972); Eugene D. Genovese, *Roll, Jordan, Roll: The World the Slaves Made* (New York, 1974); Herbert G. Gutman, *The Black Family in Slavery and Freedom, 1750–1925* (New York, 1976); Lawrence W. Levine, *Black Culture and Black Consciousness: Afro-American Folk Thought from Slavery to Freedom* (New York, 1977); Nathan Huggins, *Black Odyssey: The Afro-American Ordeal in Slavery* (New York, 1977); Litwack, *Been in the Storm So Long.*

42. See, for example, Berlin et al., *Freedom;* Lawrence N. Powell, *New Masters: Northern Planters during the Civil War and Reconstruction* (New Haven, 1980); Barbara Fields, *Slavery and Freedom on the Middle Ground: Maryland during the Nineteenth Century* (New Haven, 1985); Foner, *Reconstruction.*

43. Genovese, *Roll, Jordan, Roll,* 97–112; Litwack, *Been in the Storm So Long,* 64–103. On "self-emancipation"

see Barbara J. Fields, "Who Freed the Slaves?" in *The Civil War: An Illustrated History*, ed. Geoffrey C. Ward, Ric Burns, and Ken Burns (New York, 1990), 178–81; James M. McPherson, "Who Freed the Slaves?" *Proceedings of the American Philosophical Society* 139 (March 1995): 1–10.

44. Litwack, *Been in the Storm So Long*, 48–50.

45. "Proceedings of the Convention of the Colored People of Virginia, Held in the City of Alexandria, August 2–5, 1865," in *Proceedings of the Black State Conventions, 1840–1865*, ed. Philip S. Foner and George E. Walker, 2 vols. (Philadelphia, 1979–80), 2:270–71; *New Orleans Tribune*, June 13, 1865; *Proceedings of the Colored People's Convention of the State of South Carolina, Held in Zion Church, Charleston, South Carolina, November 1865* (Charleston, 1865), 17; Colored Mass Meeting, Norfolk, Virginia, December 1, 1865, Record Group 92, ser. 225, Central Records, National Archives, Washington, D.C.; Litwack, *Been in the Storm So Long*, 48–49.

46. Hilary McD. Beckles, "Caribbean Anti-Slavery: The Self-Liberation Ethos of Enslaved Blacks," *Journal of Caribbean History* 22 (1988): 1–19. Also see Gordon K. Lewis, *Main Currents in Caribbean Thought: The Historical Evolution of Caribbean Society in Its Ideological Aspects, 1492–1900* (Baltimore, 1983), 171–238; Viotti da Costa, *Crowns of Glory, Tears of Blood*; Reis, *Slave Rebellion in Brazil*; Ranajit Guha, *Elementary Aspects of*

Peasant Insurgency in Colonial India (Delhi, 1983); James C. Scott, *Domination and the Arts of Resistance: Hidden Transcripts* (New Haven, 1990); Florencia Mallon, *Peasant and Nation: The Making of Postcolonial Mexico and Peru* (Berkeley, Calif., 1995); John K. Thornton, *Africa and Africans in the Making of the Atlantic World, 1400–1800* (New York, 1998).

3. Marcus Garvey, the UNIA, and the Hidden Political History of African Americans

1. Information on the present-day divisions of the UNIA may be found on the organization's Web site, www.unia-acl.org, where there are links to further local information.

2. See, for example, E. David Cronon, *Black Moses: The Story of Marcus Garvey and the Universal Negro Improvement Association* (Madison, Wisc., 1955); Tony Martin, *Race First: The Ideological and Organizational Struggles of Marcus Garvey and the Universal Negro Improvement Association* (1976; rept., Dover, Mass., 1986); Judith Stein, *The World of Marcus Garvey: Race and Class in Modern Society* (Baton Rouge, 1986); Wilson Jeremiah Moses, *The Golden Age of Black Nationalism, 1850–1925* (Hamden, Conn., 1978); Lawrence W. Levine, "Marcus Garvey and the Politics of Revitalization," in *Black Leaders of the Twentieth Century,* ed. John Hope Franklin and August Meier (Urbana, Ill., 1982), 105–38; and Robert A. Hill et al., eds.,

The Marcus Garvey and Universal Negro Improvement Association Papers, 10 vols. (Berkeley, Calif., 1983–2006).

3. A new biography of Garvey has just appeared: Colin Grant, *Negro with a Hat: The Rise and Fall of Marcus Garvey and His Dream of Mother Africa* (New York, 2008). The last scholarly biography, E. David Cronon's *Black Moses,* was published in 1955.

4. See, especially, Mary Gambrell Rolinson, "The Universal Negro Improvement Association in Georgia," in *Georgia in Black and White,* ed. John Inscoe (Athens, Ga., 1994), 202–24; Mary G. Rolinson, *Grassroots Garveyism: The U.N.I.A. in the Rural South* (Chapel Hill, 2007); Barbara Bair, "Garveyism and Contested Political Terrain in 1920s Virginia," in *Afro-Virginian History and Culture,* ed. John Saillant (New York, 1999).

5. There does, however, seem to be a developing interest in the Garvey movement and popular responses to it. See, for example, Martin Summers, *Manliness and Its Discontents: The Black Middle Class and the Transformation of Masculinity, 1900–1930* (Chapel Hill, 2004); Ula Yvette Taylor, *The Veiled Garvey: The Life and Times of Amy Jacques Garvey* (Chapel Hill, 2002); Ibrahim Sundiata, *Brothers and Strangers: Black Zion, Black Slavery, 1914–1940* (Durham, N.C., 2003); Michelle Ann Stephens, *Black Empire: The Masculine Global Imaginary of Caribbean Intellectuals in the*

United States (Durham, N.C., 2005); Jahi U. Issa, "The Universal Negro Improvement Association in Louisiana: Creating a Provisional Government in Exile" (Ph.D. diss., Howard University, 2005); Claudrena N. Harold, *The Rise and Fall of the Garvey Movement in the Urban South, 1918–1942* (New York, 2007); and Jarod Roll, "Road to the Promised Land: Rural Rebellion in the New Cotton South, 1890–1945" (Ph.D. diss., Northwestern University, 2006). For the significance of the UNIA's religious appeal, see Randall K. Burkett, *Garveyism as a Religious Movement: The Institutionalization of a Black Civil Religion* (Lanham, Md., 1978).

6. Claude Andrew Clegg III, *An Original Man: The Life and Times of Elijah Muhammad* (New York, 1997); Malcolm X, *The Autobiography of Malcolm X,* as told to Alex Haley (1964; rept., New York, 1987), 1–2; John Hope Franklin, foreword to Cronon, *Black Moses,* xvii; Helen Bradford, *A Taste of Freedom: The ICU in Rural South Africa, 1924–1930* (New Haven, 1987), 213–45; Michael O. West, "The Seeds Are Sown: The Impact of Garveyism in Zimbabwe in the Interwar Years," *International Journal of African Historical Studies* 35 (2002): 335–62; Amanda D. Kemp and Robert Trent Vinson, " 'Poking Holes in the Sky': James Thaele, American Negroes, and Modernity in 1920s Segregationist South Africa," *African Studies Review* 43 (April 2000): 141–59; Michael C. Dawson, *Black*

Visions: The Roots of Contemporary African-American Political Ideologies (Chicago, 2001); John Langston Gwaltney, *Drylongso: A Self-Portrait of Black America* (New York, 1980). It is very difficult to compare the popular bases of the UNIA and the NAACP, especially because the records of the UNIA are so limited on this account. And the NAACP would see extremely impressive growth between the 1930s and the end of the Second World War, at which point the UNIA was a shell of its former self. But in the late 1910s and 1920s, the UNIA would certainly have rivaled if not surpassed the NAACP in popular support, and it probably had a more substantial following among black workers, rural and urban.

7. See *Chicago Defender,* September 6, 1919; "Interview with W. E. B. DuBois by Charles Mowbray White," August 22, 1920, and "Interview with Frederick Moore by Charles Mowbray White," both in Hill et al., *Garvey and UNIA Papers,* 2:620, 622–23; W. E. B. Du Bois, "Marcus Garvey," *Crisis* 123 (January 1921): 114–15; Phyllis R. Denbo, "The Response of the Negro Intellectual to Marcus Garvey and His Movement" (M.A. thesis, University of Pennsylvania, 1969), 29–45; Harold Cruse, *The Crisis of the Negro Intellectual: A Historical Analysis of the Failure of Black Leadership* (New York, 1967), 115–46. Thus, E. David Cronon describes some of Garvey's staunchest supporters as southern blacks who had recently mi-

grated to the North, "poorly educated, supersti-
tious, disillusioned." See Cronon, *Black Moses,* 27.

8. The UNIA divisions in New York City may have had
between 25,000 and 30,000 members in the early
1920s. For some information on the size of the large
urban divisions, see Hill et al., *Garvey and UNIA Papers,* 2:397, 410, 496, 3:163, 175–76, 252, 419, 495.

9. Estimates of the *Negro World*'s circulation range between 60,000 and 200,000. See Cronon, *Black Moses,*
44–46. On Garvey's tour see Martin, *Race First,* 8–9,
and Grant, *Negro with a Hat,* 73–86.

10. On UNIA divisions outside the United States, see
Hill et al., *Garvey and UNIA Papers,* 7:997–1000; Tony
Martin, "Marcus Garvey and Trinidad, 1912–1947,"
Arnold Hughes, "Africa and the Garvey Movement
in the Interwar Years," G. O. Olusanya, "Garvey and
Nigeria," all in *Garvey: Africa, Europe, the Americas,*
ed. Rupert Lewis and Maureen Warner-Lewis (Tren-
ton, N.J., 1994), 47–78, 99–134; Robert A. Hill and
Gregory A. Pirio, " 'Africa for the Africans': The
Garvey Movement in South Africa, 1920–1940," in
*The Politics of Race, Class, and Nationalism in Twentieth-
Century South Africa,* ed. Shula Marks and Stanley
Trapido (London, 1987), 209–53; West, "Seeds Are
Sown." On efforts to ban the distribution of the
Negro World, see Samuel A. Duncan to Earl Curzon,
January 8, 1920, in Hill et al., *Garvey and UNIA Pa-
pers,* 2:188–99; W. F. Elkins, "Marcus Garvey, the *Ne-

gro World, and the British West Indies, 1919-1920," in Lewis and Warner-Lewis, *Garvey,* 33-46. On how the *Negro World* circulated, see *La Nation Belge,* June 25, 1921, in Hill et al., *Garvey and UNIA Papers,* 9:46.

As for the geographical distribution of the divisions outside the United States, 18 were in Africa, 21 in Canada, 9 in South America, 5 in Great Britain, and 168 in Central America and the Caribbean basin, including 39 in Panama, 29 in Trinidad, 23 in Costa Rica, 26 in Cuba, and 10 in Jamaica.

11. For the number of divisions in individual states, see Hill et al., *Garvey and UNIA Papers,* 7:1001-2. The division cards on file at the Schomburg Center for Research in Black Culture encompass only the years 1926-27. Hill's figures also include what he was able to add from reports in the *Negro World* published between 1921 and 1933.

12. Membership in the urban divisions of the South appears to have swelled rapidly after they were first organized in the late 1910s or very early 1920s. Miami quickly had about 1,000 members, New Orleans had about 2,500, and the Newport News area may have had between 3,000 and 4,000. See Harold, *Rise and Fall of the Garvey Movement,* 30-31, 66-67, 93.

13. See Hill et al., *Garvey and UNIA Papers,* 7:986-96; Records of the U.N.I.A. Central Division, Manuscript 20, Boxes 22b-c, Schomburg Center for Research in Black Culture, New York City.

14. On the UNIA's requirements for divisions and membership, see "Constitution and Book of Laws," in Hill et al., *Garvey and UNIA Papers,* 1:257, 265, 266, 269. For the distribution of UNIA divisions, see Records of the Central Division, Manuscript 20, Boxes 22a–c, Schomburg Center; Hill et al., *Garvey and UNIA Papers,* 7:986–1000; Martin, *Race First,* 15–16; Winston James, *Holding Aloft the Banner of Ethiopia: Caribbean Radicalism in Early Twentieth-Century America* (London, 1998), 365–66. There are small differences in the total numbers of divisions reported in each of these sources owing to the different moments at which they became available. There is information on division memberships in the index-card boxes at the Schomburg, but it is uneven and covers only the period between 1926 and 1928. Still, it demonstrates that urban divisions, such as those in Atlanta, New Orleans, Charleston, Mobile, Richmond, Newport News, and Tampa, generally had the largest number of members.

15. *Negro World,* September 22, 1923, August 2, 1924, August 4, 1923. On the population figures, see U.S. Bureau of the Census, *Fourteenth Census of the United States: Population* (Washington, D.C., 1921), 1:191, 194, 242.

16. Report by Bureau Agent H. J. Lennbairon, October 1–2, 1920, in Hill et al., *Garvey and UNIA Papers,* 3:41–43; *Baltimore Observer,* May 1920, ibid., 2:344;

Kimberley L. Phillips, *AlabamaNorth: African-American Migrants, Community, and Working-Class Activism in Cleveland, 1915–1945* (Urbana, Ill., 1999), 186–87; Joe William Trotter, Jr. *Black Milwaukee: The Making of an Industrial Proletariat, 1915–1945* (Urbana, Ill., 1985), 124–25; Bair, "Garveyism and Contested Political Terrain in 1920s Virginia," 227–49; Earl Lewis, *In Their Own Interests: Race, Class, and Power in Twentieth-Century Norfolk, Virginia* (Berkeley, Calif., 1993); Emory Tolbert, "Outpost Garveyism and the U.N.I.A.: Rank and File," *Journal of Black Studies* 5 (March 1975): 233–53; Rolinson, *Grassroots Garveyism,* 48–71, 103–32; Roll, "Road to the Promised Land," chap. 2.

17. See, for example, Garvey Speech, March 12, 1921, in Hill et al., *Garvey and UNIA Papers,* 3:210; Garvey Editorial Letter, November 1, 1920, ibid., 68; Garvey Address, August 25, 1919, ibid., 1:502.

18. *Negro World,* November 13, 1920; "Advice of the Negro People to the Peace Conference," November 30, 1918, in Hill et al., *Garvey and UNIA Papers,* 1:303; *West Indian,* February 28, 1919, ibid., 374–75.

19. *Negro World,* July 19, 1919, November 11, 1919, March 3, 1920; Tolbert, "Outpost Garveyism," 238. As a measure of Garvey's identification with the cause of Irish nationalism, he not only corresponded with Eamon de Valera, a participant in the 1916 Easter Rising and then leader of the Irish Republic, but

also named the UNIA's meeting place (Liberty Hall) and its newspaper after their Irish republican counterparts (Liberty Hall in Dublin and the *Irish World*).

20. "Constitution and Book of Laws," July 1918, in Hill et al., *Garvey and UNIA Papers,* 1:257–75; "Amended Constitution" and "Declaration of Rights," August 1920, ibid., 2:576–77, 677–81; Garvey Speech, September 20, 1920, and Garvey Speech, September 26, 1920, ibid., 3:24–25, 28; *Negro World,* February 1, 1919, August 13, 1921; Taylor, *Veiled Garvey,* 41–42.

21. Report by Special Agent P-138, September 24, 1920, in Hill et al., *Garvey and UNIA Papers,* 3:15; Martin, *Race First,* 151–60. See also Reports by Special Agent W.W., February 26, 1920, in Hill et al., *Garvey and UNIA Papers,* 2:216.

22. See especially Stein, *World of Marcus Garvey.*

23. See Hill et al., introduction to *Garvey and UNIA Papers,* 1:xxxvi–lxxxix; Moses, *The Golden Age of Black Nationalism;* Cronon, *Black Moses,* 202–24; Eric Sundquist, *To Wake the Nations: Race in the Making of American Literature* (Cambridge, Mass., 1993), 540–625; Michele Mitchell, *Righteous Propagation: African Americans and the Politics of Racial Destiny after Reconstruction* (Chapel Hill, 2004). The cultural and political genealogy should include black freemasonry as well. See Summers, *Manliness and Its Discontents,* 17–148.

24. *Negro World,* June 13, 1925 (emphasis added). I have written at length on this impulse to self-governance in my book *A Nation under Our Feet: Black Political Struggles in the Rural South from Slavery to the Great Migration* (Cambridge, Mass., 2003).

25. See, for example, U.S. Senate, *Report and Testimony of the Select Committee of the United States Senate to Investigate the Causes of the Removal of the Negroes from the Southern States to the Northern States,* Senate Report no. 693, 46th Congress, 2nd sess. (Washington, D.C., 1880), 2:214–19, 237, 3:1–2, 433–34; *New Orleans Weekly Louisianian,* November 15, 1879, January 1, 1881; *Brenham (Texas) Weekly Banner,* June 20, 1879; Polk and Gillespie to William Coppinger, January 27, 1878, Papers of the American Colonization Society, Incoming Correspondence, Roll 117, Library of Congress, Washington, D.C.; William Mohr to Coppinger, March 6, 1880, Papers of the American Colonization Society, Incoming Correspondence, Roll 120. On grassroots emigrationism more generally, see Hahn, *A Nation under Our Feet,* 317–63; Nell I. Painter, *Exodusters: Black Migration to Kansas after Reconstruction* (New York, 1976); William Cohen, *At Freedom's Edge: Black Mobility and the Southern White Quest for Racial Control, 1861–1915* (Baton Rouge, 1991), 138–97.

26. L. G. Goodwin to William Coppinger, January 10, 1880, Papers of American Colonization Society, In-

coming Correspondence, Roll 120. Hundreds of applications for transportation and resettlement came into the offices of the American Colonization Society during the post–Civil War years, often from poor and landless communities of southern blacks. The society had customarily offered black emigrants ship's passage, several months of support, and land in Liberia, though the effects of the 1870s depression forced the society to cut back assistance dramatically, shifting most of the costs to the emigrants themselves. What's more, ships headed for Liberia departed only two or three times a year on no fixed schedule, which gave prospective emigrants little chance to finish out labor contracts, assemble money and other resources, and get to the departure points. See, for example, *African Repository* 41 (September 1865): 284; *African Repository* 49 (February 1873): 40; *African Repository* 51 (April 1875): 56; *African Repository* 56 (January 1880): 22. Migration to Kansas or Indiana was more feasible, but neither land nor employment was easy to come by, especially for groups, as opposed to individual adults or single families. See Painter, *Exodusters,* 148–53; Robert G. Athearn, *In Search of Canaan: Black Migration to Kansas, 1879–1880* (Lawrence, Kans., 1978), 78–79, 173–77; Cohen, *At Freedom's Edge,* 169, 187–94, 196, 301–11.

27. On some of the early colonies and towns in the South and then in Kansas, see Joe A. Mobley, "In the Shadow of White Society: Princeville, a Black Town in North Carolina, 1865–1915," *North Carolina Historical Review* 63 (July 1986): 340–78; Sydney Nathans, "Fortress without Walls: A Black Community after Slavery," in *Holding on to the Land and the Lord: Ritual, Land Tenure, and Social Policy in the Rural South,* ed. Robert L. Hall and Carol Stack (Athens, Ga., 1982), 55–65; Athearn, *In Search of Canaan,* 69–88. On the later and better-known black towns, see Elizabeth Rauh Bethel, *Promiseland: A Century of Life in a Negro Community* (Philadelphia, 1981); Norman L. Crockett, *The Black Towns* (Lawrence, Kans., 1979); Murray R. Wickett, *Contested Territory: Whites, Native Americans, and African Americans in Oklahoma, 1865–1907* (Baton Rouge, 2000), 30–34; Neil McMillen, *Dark Journey: Black Mississippians in the Age of Jim Crow* (Urbana, Ill., 1989), 186–88; John C. Willis, *Forgotten Time: The Yazoo-Mississippi Delta after the Civil War* (Charlottesville, Va., 2000), 71–73; Carter G. Woodson, *The Rural Negro* (Washington, D.C., 1930), 110–30.

28. See Thad Sitton and James H. Conrad, *Freedom Colonies: Independent Black Texans in the Time of Jim Crow* (Austin, Tex., 2005).

29. W. E. B. Du Bois, *The Souls of Black Folk* (1903; rept.,

New York, 1986), 443–45, 448–49, 458–74; Chalmers
Archer Jr., *Growing Up Black in Rural Mississippi: Memories of a Family, Heritage of a Place* (New York, 1992).

30. See Hahn, *A Nation under Our Feet*, 317–63, 465–76;
Rolinson, *Grassroots Garveyism*, 48–71; Barbara
Ransby, *Ella Baker and the Black Freedom Movement:
A Radical Democratic Vision* (Chapel Hill, 2003), 13–45.
On the first reparations movement, see Mary Frances Berry's powerful *My Face Is Black Is True: Callie
House and the Struggle for Ex-Slave Reparations* (New
York, 2005).

31. Nan Elizabeth Woodruff, *American Congo: The Black
Freedom Struggle in the Arkansas and Mississippi Delta,
1900–1950* (Cambridge, Mass., 2005), 74–190; Jeannie
Whayne, *A New Plantation South: Land, Labor, and
Federal Favor in Twentieth-Century Arkansas* (Charlottesville, Va., 1996), 47–77; M. Langley Biegert,
"Legacy of Resistance: Uncovering the History of
Collective Action by Black Agricultural Workers in
Central East Arkansas from the 1860s to the 1930s,"
Journal of Social History 32 (Fall 1998): 73–99.

32. Woodruff, *American Congo*, 74–109; Drive Director
to Lee L. Brown, March 23, 1921, Papers of the
NAACP, Part 12, ser. A, Roll 11, Library of Congress,
Washington, D.C.; *Branch Bulletin*, April 1919, Papers
of the NAACP, Part 12, ser. A, Roll 11; Steven Reich,
"Soldiers of Democracy: Black Texans and the
Fight for Citizenship, 1917–1921," *Journal of American*

History 82 (March 1996): 1492–1501; Greta de Jong, *A Different Day: African-American Struggles for Justice in Rural Louisiana, 1900–1970* (Chapel Hill, 2002), 67–68. Also see Patricia A. Sullivan, *American Dream: The NAACP and the Struggle for Civil Rights* (forthcoming).

33. Hill et al., *Garvey and UNIA Papers,* 7:986–95.

34. See Jarod Roll's outstanding treatment of the Missouri story in "Road to the Promised Land," chap. 2. Also see Rolinson, *Grassroots Garveyism,* 178–79.

35. For thoughtful objections to political and intellectual oppositions such as these, see Nikhil Pal Singh, *Black Is a Country: Race and the Unfinished Struggle for Democracy* (Cambridge, Mass., 2004).

36. We are, however, beginning to pay more attention to these traditions. See, for example, Timothy Tyson, *Radio Free Dixie: Robert F. Williams and the Roots of Black Power* (Chapel Hill, 1999); Lance Hill, *The Deacons for Defense: Armed Resistance and the Civil Rights Movement* (Chapel Hill, 2004).

37. See Daniel Dalrymple, "In the Shadow of Garvey: Garveyites in the United States and the British Caribbean, 1930–1945" (Ph.D. diss., Michigan State University, 2008); interviews with Thomas W. Harvey and John Vincent, in *Footsoldiers of the Universal Negro Improvement Association: Their Own Words,* ed. Jeannette Smith-Irvin (Trenton, N.J., 1989), 26–27, 53–55; Harold, *Rise and Fall of the Garvey Movement,* 109–20. See also Thomas Sugrue's ex-

traordinary *Sweet Land of Liberty: The Forgotten Struggle for Civil Rights in the North* (New York, 2008). Joe W. Trotter, Jr. shows both that the UNIA in Milwaukee lived on after Garvey's personal downfall and that its leaders became involved in municipal politics; see *Black Milwaukee: The Making of an Industrial Proletariat, 1915–1945* (Urbana, Ill., 1985), 134–35.

38. Clegg, *An Original Man,* 100; Amy Jacques Garvey, *Garvey and Garveyism,* introduction by John Henrik Clarke (New York, 1963), 305; Regina Freer, "L.A. Race Woman: Charlotta Bass and the Complexities of Black Political Development in Los Angeles," *American Quarterly* 56 (September 2004): 607–20; Jeanne Theoharis, " 'Alabama on Avalon': Rethinking the Watts Uprising and the Character of Black Protest in Los Angeles," in *The Black Power Movement: Rethinking the Civil Rights–Black Power Era,* ed. Peniel Joseph (New York, 2006), 32, 46. Elijah Muhammad was born in rural Georgia in 1897 before moving on to Macon, Georgia, and then Detroit.

39. For Sylvia Woods and Randolph Blackwell, see Harold, *Rise and Fall of the Garvey Movement,* 118–20, 122–23; Alice Lynd and Staughton Lynd, eds., *Rank and File: Personal Histories by Working-Class Organizers* (Boston, 1973), 111–29.

40. For James Anderson and Queen Mother Audley

Moore, see Harold, *Rise and Fall of the Garvey Movement*, 120–21, 123–24. It is worth adding that William Henry Moses, the Baptist minister and Garvey supporter, was the grandfather of Bob Moses, the important grassroots leader in the Civil Rights movement. On William Moses see Burkett, *Garveyism as a Religious Movement*, 117–22.

41. Eddie Glaude, introduction, and Robin D. G. Kelley, "Stormy Weather: Reconstructing Black (Inter)Nationalism in the Cold War Era," both in *Is It Nation Time?: Contemporary Essays on Black Power and Nationalism*, ed. Eddie Glaude (Chicago, 2002), 4–5, 67–90; Peniel Joseph, *Waiting 'Til the Midnight Hour: A Narrative History of Black Power in America* (New York, 2006), 11–12; Malcolm X, *The Autobiography of Malcolm X*, 4–10, 151–90; Garvey, *Garvey and Garveyism*, 307–8; Kwame Nkrumah, *Ghana: The Autobiography of Kwame Nkrumah* (London, 1957), 45.

42. When the UNIA established a division in Key West, Florida, in 1920, a Ku Klux Klan chapter was quickly organized in response. UNIA organizers were also harassed in Texas and Alabama, but in general it appears that local divisions of the UNIA either were unknown to whites or did not provoke them. On harassment, see Martin, *Race First*, 345.

43. See, for example, Summers, *Manliness and Its Discontents*, 66–148; Mitchell, *Righteous Propagation*, 218–39;

James, *Holding Aloft the Banner of Ethiopia,* 122–94; Taylor, *The Veiled Garvey;* Stephens, *Black Empire,* 75–125.

44. There have been a number of excellent studies of developing nationalist sensibilities in this period, but they have focused chiefly on the middle, or "respectable," classes, or on important intellectuals. See, for example, Singh, *Black Is a Country;* Kevin K. Gaines, *Uplifting the Race: Black Leadership, Politics, and Culture in the Twentieth Century* (Chapel Hill, 1996); Mitchell, *Righteous Propagation.* Little attention has been devoted to popular forms of nationalism, especially those carried out of the South.

45. Du Bois, "Marcus Garvey," 60; *Crisis* 123 (January 1921): 114–15; W. E. B. Du Bois to Editor, *New York Age,* June 25, 1921, in Hill et al., *Garvey and UNIA Papers,* 3:480; "Interview with Frederick Moore," Ibid., 2:620; W. E. B. Du Bois to Charles Evans Hughes, January 5, 1923, and W. E. B. Du Bois to W. A. Domingo, January 18, 1923, in *The Correspondence of W. E. B. Du Bois,* ed. Herbert Aptheker, 3 vols. (Amherst, Mass., 1973), 1:261–64.

46. The challenges include a number of outstanding studies of black community development. See, for example, Trotter, *Black Milwaukee;* Lewis, *In Their Own Interests;* James R. Grossman, *Land of Hope: Chicago, Black Southerners, and the Great Migration* (Chicago, 1989); Robin D. G. Kelley, *Hammer and Hoe: Al-*

abama Communists during the Great Depression (Chapel Hill, 1990); Tera Hunter, *To 'Joy My Freedom: Southern Black Women's Lives and Labors after the Civil War* (Cambridge, Mass., 1997); Thomas J. Sugrue, *The Origins of the Urban Crisis: Race and Inequality in Postwar Detroit* (Princeton, 1996); Phillips, *AlabamaNorth;* Victoria W. Wolcott, *Remaking Respectability: African American Women in Interwar Detroit* (Chapel Hill, 2001). The challenges also include new treatments of Black Power, black nationalism, and armed self-defense. See Joseph, *Waiting 'Til the Midnight Hour;* Joseph, *The Black Power Movement;* Hill, *Deacons for Defense;* Tyson, *Radio Free Dixie;* Dawson, *Black Visions;* Tommie Shelby, *We Who Are Dark: The Philosophical Foundations of Black Solidarity* (Cambridge, Mass., 2005); Robin D. G. Kelley, *Freedom Dreams: The Black Radical Imagination* (Boston, 2002); Robin D. G. Kelley, *Race Rebels: Culture, Politics, and the Black Working Class* (New York, 1996); Glaude, *Is It Nation Time?;* William L. Van Deburg, *New Day in Babylon: The Black Power Movement and American Culture, 1965–1975* (Chicago, 1992).

ACKNOWLEDGMENTS

First and foremost, I should like to express my deepest thanks to Henry Louis Gates Jr. and Evelyn Brooks Higginbotham for extending what I regard to be one of the great honors in American intellectual life: an invitation to deliver the Nathan I. Huggins Lectures at Harvard. I should like to thank them too for their incredible hospitality and for helping make my experience as Huggins Lecturer not only extremely stimulating but also a great deal of fun. I am very grateful, as well, to Walter Johnson and Bill McFeely for their overly generous introductions, and to William Julius Wilson, Tommy Shelby, Linda Heywood, John K. Thornton, and others in the audience (including Skip Gates and Evelyn Higginbotham) for their tough questions and general encouragement. This book is, I hope, better for their engagement, even if it doesn't fully satisfy all their doubts.

Neither the lectures nor the book manuscript would have been completed in a timely fashion had it not been for important help I received along the way. The dean's office in the School of Arts and Sciences at the University of Pennsylvania provided me with crucial leave time, and three outstanding Penn graduate students—Matt Karp, Will Kuby, and Tshepo Masango—gave me a hand with the research. I have had the opportunity to try out some of my ideas at the University of Toronto, Princeton University, the University of California, San Diego, the University of Texas, Michigan State University, Tulane University, Yale University, and the University of Rochester, and at the annual meeting of the Southern Intellectual History Circle, and I very much appreciate both the enthusiasm and the skepticism expressed by those in attendance. I have also been able to call on a number of good friends who were willing to take time from their own work to assist me with mine and to offer extremely helpful criticism as well as the confidence to go ahead with the risks I wished to take: Ira Berlin, Larry Powell, Jonathan Prude, Tom Summerhill, and Tom Sugrue.

I have had the great good fortune to work again with Joyce Seltzer of the Harvard University Press, whose enthusiasm, encouragement, and insight have been invaluable. Stephanie McCurry helped me develop many of the ideas in this book both in ongoing conversations and through her own remarkable scholarship—soon to be published—on the complex political worlds of the Confederate South.

My son, Declan, and daughter, Saoirse, have been very good sports about putting up with a family life in which both their parents always seem to be re-searching, writing, and talking about history and poli-tics. But more inspiring to me, they have emerged as endlessly curious and exceptionally vibrant citizens of the world: savvy, sophisticated, and, most impor-tant of all, good and warm-hearted. With love, joy, and eyes to the future, I dedicate this book to them.

Index